CW00971435

ADAM LIAW'S
ASIAN COOKERY SCHOOL

⊞ hachette
AUSTRALIA

First published in Australia and New Zealand in 2015
by Hachette Australia
(an imprint of Hachette Australia Pty Limited)
Level 17, 207 Kent Street, Sydney NSW 2000
www.hachette.com.au

This edition published in 2017

10 9 8 7 6 5 4 3 2 1

Copyright © Adam Liaw 2015

This book is copyright. Apart from any fair dealing for the purposes of private
study, research, criticism or review permitted under the *Copyright Act 1968*, no
part may be stored or reproduced by any process without prior written permission.
Enquiries should be made to the publisher.

National Library of Australia
Cataloguing-in-Publication data:

Liaw, Adam, author.

Adam Liaw's Asian cookery school/Adam Liaw.

978 0 7336 3930 2 (paperback)

Cooking, Asian

641.595

Jacket and internal design by Liz Seymour/Seymour Designs
Photography by Steve Brown
Food styling by Berni Smithies
Food preparation by Olivia Andrews
Typeset in 9.5/13 Interstate light by Seymour Designs
Printed in China by 1010 Printing International

FOR MY DAD, WHO TAUGHT
ME EVERYTHING I KNOW

CONTENTS

INTRODUCTION

I love Asian food.

When I was a kid, my brother Aron and I would always order Crispy Skin Chicken at our local Chinese restaurant. Every time. We would argue over what spices we thought were in the five-spice salt, and fight over whether the thigh or wing was the best part of the bird (the thigh was always juicier, but the wing had more of the crispy skin). We would wonder how they got the skin so crispy, and my parents or grandma would chime in with a piece of sage advice now and then.

After a hundred conversations over a hundred dinners I knew Crispy Skin Chicken inside and out long before I ever thought to make it myself. You can find my recipe now on page 175.

I ate a thousand pieces of bad sushi (and loved them) before I had my first good piece and never looked back. Then I probably ate a thousand more pieces of good sushi before I picked up a sushi mat for the first time. If you want to give it a try, there are a couple of classic rolls on page 103.

If you love to eat Asian food, knowing how to cook it is a natural and important progression. In this book I want to teach you all about Asian food – not just how to cook it, but also how to understand it and appreciate it.

Food does not exist on its own. It goes hand-in-hand with culture and experience, and to try and separate food from those things or to reduce it to just a list of ingredients and a method in a written recipe, would be to only tell half the story. As you follow the recipes in this book also follow the stories and context around them. Those are equally important.

My education in food didn't just come from repeating recipes over and over (although that was certainly part of it). When I first learned to cook from my parents and grandparents they passed me their knowledge with a comment here, a guided hand there, and even a laugh or a sharp word when it was needed. I learned more from the hundreds of tips and small wisdoms that my family and friends passed to me over the years than I ever could have learned from recipes alone. Those moments taught me how to think about food.

I often hear people say that they don't need to learn how to cook Asian food because they just eat it at restaurants where it's easy and affordable. That's a reasonable sentiment, but one that I think misses the point.

The food I love is personal and important to me, and I don't think I could ever completely hand over something so important to a stranger I will never meet, working out the back of a restaurant. Don't get me wrong; I love going out to eat, but I wouldn't consider it a substitute for the experience of home cooking.

You can buy a hamburger for just a few dollars in just about every country in the world, but if you love hamburgers does that mean you should never learn how to make one? Asian food is cheap and readily available, and yet all through Asia people still cook it at home every single day.

Home-cooked food is more than just a tasty meal. It's an experience, a process, an achievement, and an expression of who you are.

I can order dumplings anywhere, but even the best dumplings from the best restaurant won't be the same as the Shui Jiao (page 106) my grandma taught me to make. The first time I cooked Chicken and Vegetable Nimono (page 58) with my wife, she told me a story of how her mother and late grandmother had shown her how to make it years before. I wouldn't give that experience up for anything.

In this book I've tried to show you more than just recipes. I've tried to show you some of the insights into Asian cookery that my family and friends have given me throughout my life. It's through those insights that I learned to cook, and I offer them to you here in the hope that you might want to learn too.

Adam Liaw

LESSON 1
A STARTING POINT

There is no such thing as a single, unified Asian cuisine. Even if we only count the countries of East and Southeast Asia, we have nearly twenty separate nations, each with their own history, language, culture and cuisine.

The breadth and variety in Asian cuisines is staggering, but even with their differences, centuries of trade, migration and shared history means we can draw some lines of consistency between them. Dishes originating in Indonesia have turned up in modern-day Okinawa, Chinese noodles are found all over the region, and even sushi – an icon of Japanese cuisine – can trace its origins back to Thailand.

In the lessons in this book I haven't tried to give you a definitive comparison of the styles of the many schools of regional Chinese cuisine, or to illustrate the differences between the food of the different provinces of Thailand. That level of detail is a story for another time.

This book is an introduction to the techniques and flavours of Asian cookery, and I've selected dishes from around the region to show you a broad and authentic impression of how people in Asia really eat. Not every dish may be to your taste, but certainly some will be. Think of this book as the start of your journey to discover Asian cookery. Right now, we're just deciding which direction to walk in.

A SHARED MEAL

An Asian meal is usually a selection of dishes placed in the centre of a table and shared among the family, often with cooked rice anchoring it all together.

Serving multiple dishes provides variety, caters for different tastes, and balances a meal. A heavy, deep-fried dish can be offset with lighter steamed dishes, meaty foods can be matched with those containing plenty of vegetables, dry dishes with soupy ones, and so on. Variety and balance should be looked at, taking the whole table into account.

Growing up in a Chinese household, I was always taught that it is good manners to serve an odd number of dishes, and never less than three.

The speed and simplicity of cooking Asian dishes suits the preparation of multiple plates. Wok-fried dishes can be cooked very quickly, and are usually far more simple than the 'stir-fries' we produce in the West. Rather than throwing twelve different ingredients into a single, confused stir-fry, a more authentically Asian way of cooking could create four distinct dishes of three ingredients each, producing a greater variety and cleaner expression of flavours.

In this book I've given you a variety of options. Some dishes like the Pork Belly, Cabbage and Shiitake Hotpot (page 13) are larger servings that can be eaten by a whole family as a single dish, or divided over a few nights as part of a shared spread. Others like the Spinach in Sesame Dressing (page 6) are smaller servings designed to be served with a few other dishes. Others still, like the Pad Thai (page 45), can be eaten as meals just on their own.

HOW TO SHARE

Sharing an Asian meal is a process that happens over time. The idea is to share the dishes, not just divide them. Don't just wait for everything to arrive on the table and then pile your plate high with your allotment of each dish. Just take one or two pieces of a dish and eat them before moving on to the next one.

For meals eaten at home, the practice is to place all the food on the table at once, and to make sure all family members are seated before starting to eat.

DESIGNING AN ASIAN MENU

If you're putting together a spread of dishes for a shared meal, try to create a natural balance of textures and ingredients. Just taking Chinese cuisine as an example, if you start with a drier fried dish like Salt and Pepper Prawns (page 90), perhaps a wetter, lighter steamed dish like Steamed Fish with Ginger and Spring Onion (page 17) might help balance. Then with those two dishes the meal has a lot of seafood, so a meaty dish like Dongpo Pork (page 193) might be a good choice. Now your menu is looking quite strongly flavoured, so a dish lighter in flavour like Oiled Greens (page 133) again restores balance.

That may sound like a good meal, but the even number of dishes sits a bit uneasily with me. Almost like a conversation, an even number of dishes can easily be paired up two by two, but for a really good conversation you want everyone to be involved, so a fifth dish like a small plate of cold White Cut Chicken (page 172) is important. Add some Cooked Rice (page 100) and the meal is complete, balanced and cohesive.

CREATING ASIAN FLAVOUR THROUGH TECHNIQUE

One of the easiest mistakes to make when getting started with Asian food is trying to make a dish too 'Asian'. Often in an attempt to take a simple ingredient away from a more familiar Western style, you might be tempted to add in too many seasonings, spices or other identifiably 'Asian' flavours. You don't need to. A chicken doesn't have a nationality, nor does a carrot. You can create a more characteristic Asian flavour by paying attention to the texture created by how you cut meat and vegetables, how you apply heat to an ingredient, and how you combine ingredients, and these will have a greater impact than any number of sauces you use.

In this first lesson you'll find simple, homely recipes from around Asia. They are the kind of recipes you might find on a family dinner table in Japan, China, Korea or Malaysia on a weeknight. In fact, they're the kind of recipes you'd find on my dinner table on a weeknight, too.

I've chosen the recipes in this lesson to show a few simple techniques that, although not unique to Asian cookery, are very important in creating Asian flavour. Steaming, braising and grinding are some of the most basic processes in cooking, so I think here's a good place to get started.

EQUIPMENT FOR AN ASIAN KITCHEN

You don't need any special equipment or ingredients to get started in Asian cookery. A dish that can be cooked in a claypot can easily be cooked in a saucepan, and any dish fried in a wok can be made in a large frypan instead. But a few simple additions to your kitchen will make preparing great Asian food a little easier. Here are a few basics:

Steamer – A steamer is used to hold individual ingredients or whole plates of food for steaming over boiling water. Steaming is a very popular style of cooking in Asian cuisines. Bamboo steamers can be placed over any wok or saucepan of appropriate size. **1**

Mortar and pestle – A mortar (the bowl) and pestle (the stick) is used to pound, crush or grind ingredients to create sauces, pastes or powders. There are many different kinds from deep, cone-like Thai mortars that are designed to lightly crush soft ingredients to ridged Japanese *suribachi* more suited for grinding. A heavy stone Chinese or Southeast Asian mortar and pestle is a good multi-purpose choice. **2**

Wok – Woks are the all-purpose cooking vessel of the Asian kitchen, used for boiling, frying, deep-frying, braising and even steaming. They originated in China but are now found all throughout Southeast Asia, Japan (where they are called a *chuka-nabe*, or Chinese pot), Korea and even India. We'll explore woks further in Lesson 4. **3**

Claypot – Often used in Southeast Asian cooking, claypots are traditionally used to produce gentle, moist and even heat for braising. A heavy, lidded saucepan or Dutch oven would make a perfect substitute. **4**

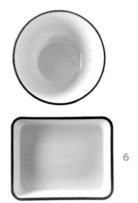

5   6   7   8

Rice cooker - Almost every Asian household would own a rice cooker, and it would be the most popular pot or appliance in the house. They are used for cooking rice of all kinds, as well as for keeping cooked rice warm for up to a day or two. **5**

Prep trays and bowls - One of the most important parts of Asian cookery is being well prepared before any actual cooking takes place. Dedicated bowls or trays for placing prepared ingredients before cooking are more necessary than you may think and are essential to good kitchen craft, avoiding overcrowded cutting boards. **6**

Cooking chopsticks - While a good pair of tongs will work nearly as well, I find cooking chopsticks very useful in the kitchen. They are usually about 1½ times the length of eating chopsticks and are uncoated, so that they can be safely heated. **7**

Japanese grater - I use my Japanese grater for grating radish, ginger and even garlic. Plastic versions are available from Asian grocers, but a rasp grater or the bumpy side of a box grater work just as well. **8**

SPINACH IN SESAME DRESSING
Horenso no gomae

MAKES 1 SERVE FOR SHARING PREPARATION TIME 10 MINS **COOKING TIME 1 MIN**

This Japanese side dish is one of the most popular accompaniments to a home-style meal and it's also a great way to get started using a mortar and pestle. You can grind the sesame as coarsely or as finely as you like.

INGREDIENTS

3 tbsp sesame seeds

2 tsp sugar

2 tsp sake

1 tsp soy sauce, plus extra for drizzling

1 bunch (about 250g) spinach

METHOD

1   Toast the sesame seeds in a dry saucepan over medium heat and transfer to a large mortar and pestle with the sugar. Grind to a rough paste then add the sake and soy sauce and continue to grind until quite smooth.

2   Wash the spinach well, keeping the roots intact. Bring a saucepan of water to a rolling boil. Place the spinach in the pot roots first and hold the roots and stems in the liquid for about 10 seconds, then lower the leaves into the water and cook for 30 seconds. Remove the spinach from the pot, drop it into a bowl of cold water to stop the cooking, then squeeze out as much liquid as possible (use a sushi mat if you like, or your hands).

3   Place the spinach on a large plate and drizzle with a little soy sauce, then cut it into 5cm lengths and discard the roots. Transfer to the mortar. Mix with the sesame dressing but do not pound the spinach. Remove from the mortar and serve at room temperature.

NOTES

A Japanese mortar (*suribachi*) has ridges inside the bowl and is used for grinding rather than pounding, but any mortar and pestle will work fine.

I prefer toasting sesame seeds in a small saucepan rather than a frypan because it allows you to swirl the seeds rather than trying to toss them in a frypan. The swirling motion will toast the seeds more evenly.

Toasting sesame seeds brings out a strong nutty flavour, but also makes them more brittle. The seeds will grind more easily when well toasted.

MUSHIBUTA
Steamed pork belly with vegetables

SERVES 2 PREPARATION TIME 15 MINS **COOKING TIME 12 MINS**

This quick and simple Japanese dish is one of my favourite dinners, both in hot weather and cold, and it makes an appearance on my dinner table at least once every couple of weeks. It's a perfect way to get to know your steamer.

INGREDIENTS

¼ Chinese cabbage, sliced into 5cm widths

1 carrot, peeled and thinly sliced

4 thick spring onions, trimmed and cut diagonally into 5cm lengths

100g enoki mushrooms, bases trimmed, separated into clumps

1 cup beansprouts

1 tsp salt

400g pork belly, skin and bone removed, sliced into ½cm strips

¼ tsp white pepper

1 cup finely grated daikon, to serve (optional)

Ponzu (page 29), to serve

METHOD

1   Place all the vegetables except the daikon directly on the base of a bamboo steamer and season with a little of the salt. Lay the pork strips on top and season with pepper and the remaining salt.

2   Bring ample water to the boil in a wok or large pot that will accommodate the steamer. When the water is boiling place the steamer on top and steam for 12 minutes.

3   Remove the lid from the steamer and transfer the whole steamer directly to the table (with a plate or tray underneath to catch drips). Gently squeeze any excess liquid from the raw grated daikon (if using) and scatter over the pork. Pour some of the Ponzu over the daikon, pork and vegetables to serve, and serve the rest of the Ponzu on the side.

NOTES

This dish is a great example of clean Asian flavour. There is no thick sauce or spicy condiments – just the natural flavours of the meat and vegetables, enhanced by a light seasoning.

If the pork is cut too thickly it won't cook properly. Your butcher should be able to cut the pork for you, but if you're cutting it yourself place the block of pork in the freezer for an hour or two to firm before cutting with a sharp knife.

Raw, finely grated daikon is used in Japanese cooking as a light and sharp foil to rich, oily or meaty dishes, or to add body to light sauces like *ponzu* or *tentsuyu*.

STEAMED GINGER CHICKEN

SERVES 4 PREPARATION TIME 10 MINS **MARINATING TIME 15 MINS** COOKING TIME 10 MINS

This home-style dish is the kind of thing my family ate all the time when I was growing up, and it's easy to see why it's a firm favourite - it's simple to make, fast and quite delicious.

INGREDIENTS

1 tbsp grated ginger

1 tbsp Shaoxing wine

1 tsp soy sauce

1 tsp cornflour

½ tsp salt

½ tsp sugar

2 thick spring onions, trimmed and finely chopped

600g chicken thigh fillets, cut into 5cm chunks

¼ cup coriander leaves, to serve

METHOD

1   Combine the ginger, Shaoxing wine, soy sauce, cornflour, salt, sugar, spring onions, and chicken pieces in a large bowl. Mix well, and set aside for at least 15 minutes.

2   Arrange the marinated chicken in a single layer on a heatproof serving plate that will fit inside your bamboo steamer. Bring plenty of water to the boil in a saucepan or wok under the steamer, place the plate of chicken inside the steamer, cover and steam for 10 minutes.

3   Remove the plate from the steamer and allow to stand for a minute. Scatter the chicken with the coriander and serve immediately.

NOTES

The chicken will release flavourful juices during cooking, so use a shallow dish with a lip to catch them. Be careful not to spill the juices when taking the dish out of the steamer.

To grate the ginger, peel it by scraping the skin away with a teaspoon and grate it as finely as possible using a Japanese grater, a rasp grater or the bumpy side of a box grater.

Coriander has flavour through the entire plant, from the roots to the leaves, and it's all edible. If you want a stronger coriander flavour in the dish, mix chopped coriander stems and roots with the chicken and steam it all together, scattering the leaves over to serve.

PORK BELLY, CABBAGE AND SHIITAKE HOTPOT

SERVES 4 PREPARATION TIME 15 MINS + 15 MINS STANDING **COOKING TIME 45 MINS**

If you can make a stew, you can make this wintery Chinese hotpot. You don't need a claypot, either. A heavy saucepan or Dutch oven will work just as well.

INGREDIENTS

8 dried shiitake mushrooms

1 tbsp vegetable oil

600g pork belly, bone removed, cut into 3cm cubes

3 cloves garlic, peeled

3 large spring onions, peeled and cut into 5cm lengths

¼ Chinese cabbage, cut into chunks

2 tbsp oyster sauce

1 tbsp Shaoxing wine

½ tsp salt

¼ tsp white pepper

1 tbsp cornflour mixed with 2 tbsp cold water

METHOD

1   Cover the dried mushrooms with 2 cups boiling water and allow to stand for 15 minutes. Remove and discard the stalks, reserving the caps and the steeping liquid.

2   Heat the vegetable oil in a claypot or large saucepan and fry the pork in batches until well browned. When the final batch is browned, return all the pork to the pot and add 1½ cups of the reserved shiitake steeping liquid. Simmer the pork, covered, for 10 minutes then add the vegetables, oyster sauce, Shaoxing wine, salt and pepper. Stir well and simmer the pork and vegetables, covered, for a further 20 minutes, or until the vegetables and meat are softened.

3   Stir the cornflour mixture through the hotpot and cook for a minute until thickened. Remove from the heat and allow to rest for 5 minutes before serving.

NOTES

The flavour in this dish comes from the strong umami taste of the browned pork, Chinese cabbage and shiitake stock. A touch of oyster sauce adds some seasoning but, as in so many Asian dishes, the trick is drawing out the natural flavours of the ingredients.

The easiest way to remove the stalks of shiitake mushrooms after soaking is to snip them off with a pair of kitchen scissors. Don't cut them off before soaking. They add a lot of flavour to the stock.

Thickening the sauce adds body to the dish as well as helping the flavourful broth coat the meat and vegetables. If the sauce is too thin, it will all lack flavour.

KOREAN BRAISED CHILLI CHICKEN
Dakdoritang

SERVES 4-6 PREPARATION TIME 15 MINS **COOKING TIME 50 MINS**

No cuisine is complete without a good chicken stew. *Dakdoritang* is Korea's spicy and sweet answer to France's *coq au vin* and Italy's *cacciatore*.

INGREDIENTS

2kg chicken wings or 1 whole chicken (about 1.6kg), cut into pieces

2 large brown onions, peeled and cut into thick slices

About 1 litre water, Anchovy Stock (page 33) or Bonito Stock (page 32)

2 medium carrots, peeled and cut into chunks

3 medium potatoes, peeled and cut into chunks

3 small spring onions, trimmed and finely sliced, to serve

Sauce

¼ cup soy sauce

¼ cup Korean chilli paste (*gochujang*)

2 tbsp Korean chilli powder (*gochugaru*)

1 tbsp caster sugar

1 tbsp honey

5 cloves garlic, peeled and minced

2 tsp grated ginger

¼ tsp salt

METHOD

1 Prepare the chicken wings by cutting through the joints to separate the drumettes, wingettes and wing tips (see pages 164-165). Reserve the wing tips for stock, and place the drumettes and wingettes in a large bowl with the onion.

2 Mix together the ingredients for the sauce and toss through the chicken and onion. Transfer the chicken, onion and sauce to a large saucepan and add enough water or stock to just cover the chicken. Bring to a simmer and simmer, covered, for 15 minutes, skimming any scum from the surface.

3 Stir in the carrots and potatoes, cover and simmer for a further 15 minutes, stirring occasionally. Uncover the pot and simmer for a further 10 minutes to reduce the liquid. Adjust for seasoning, scatter over the spring onions and serve.

NOTES

Dishes taste better when meat or poultry is cooked on the bone. Not only does the bone provide flavour like it does to a stock, but the meat doesn't shrink as much during cooking, keeping it more tender.

Korean cuisine often uses multiple sources of the same kind of flavour to provide greater complexity to a dish. Just taking sweetness as an example, here we have four sources of sweetness - sugar, honey, *gochujang* and natural sweetness from the vegetables themselves. We'll discuss this further in the next lesson.

STEAMED FISH WITH GINGER AND SPRING ONION

SERVES 4 PREPARATION TIME 10 MINS **COOKING TIME 10 MINS**

The more traditional version of this Cantonese classic uses a whole fish, but if you're just starting out with Asian food, fillets are an easier option.

INGREDIENTS

600g skinless white fish fillets, such as snapper, bones removed

¼ tsp salt

1 tbsp soy sauce

1 tbsp Shaoxing wine

A pinch sugar (optional)

2cm ginger, peeled and finely shredded, or 1 tbsp grated ginger

2 thick spring onions, trimmed and finely shredded

2 tbsp peanut oil

½ cup loosely packed coriander leaves, to serve

METHOD

1 Place your steamer over a pot of water over medium heat and bring to the boil.

2 Season the fish all over with salt and place in a shallow dish that will fit inside your steamer. Mix together the soy sauce, wine, and sugar (if using) and pour over the fish. Scatter with half the ginger. Place the dish in the steamer, cover and steam for 7 minutes. You can check if the fish is done by squeezing the fillets with your fingers. They should feel firm and flaky, so if you squeezed harder the fillet would break along its natural grain.

3 Remove the fish from the steamer, scatter with the remaining ginger and the spring onion and spoon the juices collected in the dish back over the fish a few times.

4 Heat the oil until smoking and carefully pour over the fish, and particularly over the raw ginger to release its flavour. Scatter with the coriander and serve.

NOTES

The ginger should be shredded very finely - no thicker than a matchstick - as it will be eaten mostly raw. If you aren't confident about cutting the ginger finely enough, use grated ginger instead.

Ginger is a common companion for fish in Asian cuisines. The idea is that ginger's sharp fragrance counteracts any fishy smell.

A pair of fish tweezers is handy for removing fine bones. Dip the tweezers in a bowl of water after removing each bone - the surface tension of the water will pull the bone from the tweezers.

NYONYA CHICKEN STEW
Ayam pongteh

SERVES 4-6 PREPARATION TIME 25 MINS **COOKING TIME 40 MINS**

You can never have too many chicken casserole recipes. This Nyonya version is from around Malacca in Malaysia. The Nyonyas are a group of ethnic Chinese who have been living in Malaysia for nearly 500 years, and their cuisine has developed into a beautiful combination of Chinese and Malay influences.

INGREDIENTS

8 dried shiitake mushrooms

5 eschalots, peeled and sliced, or 2 small brown onions, peeled and roughly chopped

5 cloves garlic, peeled

¼ cup vegetable oil

1 whole chicken (1.6kg), cut into pieces, or 1kg chicken thigh fillets, cut into 5cm pieces

¼ cup fermented yellow beans, or miso paste

½ tsp salt

1 tbsp dark soy sauce

2 tsp soy sauce

1 tbsp sugar

4 medium potatoes, peeled and cut into 5cm chunks

Cooked rice and Sambal Belacan (page 28), to serve

METHOD

1   Soak the mushrooms in 2 cups of hot water for 20 minutes, or until softened. Remove the stems and discard, but reserve the steeping water.

2   Pound the eschalots and garlic together with a mortar and pestle, or purée in a food processor. Add the oil to a hot wok over medium heat, add the purée and fry, stirring regularly for about 5 minutes, or until the ingredients are fragrant and the oil separates from the solids.

3   Add the chicken pieces, fermented beans or miso paste and salt and fry until the chicken is coated in the purée and starting to brown. Add the mushrooms and toss to coat. Add the dark soy sauce, soy sauce and sugar, 1½ cups of the reserved shiitake liquid and 1½ cups water. Cover the wok and simmer for 15 minutes.

4   Add the potatoes and simmer, uncovered, for a further 15 minutes, stirring occasionally until the potatoes are softened and the sauce has thickened. Serve with rice and Sambal Belacan.

NOTES

The purée of onions and garlic here is a very basic *rempah*, or spice paste. *Rempah* is very important to Malaysian cooking in the same way that *mirepoix* is to French or *sofrito* to Spanish food. It provides a base of flavour and the puréed onion also helps thicken the final dish. The secret with any *rempah* is to cook out the water, leaving a strong flavour base.

Malaysian cuisine is a cultural mix of Malay, Chinese and Indian influences. As a Muslim country, much of Malaysian cuisine is *halal*, although the foods characteristic of Malaysia's non-Muslim ethnic Chinese community often contain pork or alcohol. Nyonya food has been around in Malaysia for centuries, and is quite different from the food of the Chinese Malaysian communities who migrated in the last hundred years or so.

LESSON 2
UNDERSTANDING FLAVOUR

When I was first learning to cook as a child, I spent a long time trying to work out how everything my grandmother made tasted so good. She would just throw a couple of ingredients into a wok, toss it around for a bit and produce a dish that was light and delicate but intensely flavourful in just a few minutes.

Trying it myself, I would load up my dishes with dozens of different combinations of sauces and seasonings in an attempt to re-create that distinctive taste, but it was never quite right. Even when I asked her how she got everything to taste so good, she would just look at me exasperatedly and show me again (and again) how she cooked. It took me years to realise where I was going wrong.

My mistake was not that I was adding the wrong ingredients; it was more fundamental than that. I had thought flavour was something you added to ingredients, but the secret to Asian cookery is that flavour is something you bring out in the ingredients themselves.

I had been looking in the cupboard for the source of my grandmother's delicious cooking, when all the time I should have been looking in the pan. She would cut the ingredients well and cook them with care, then add seasonings with a light hand just to enhance the natural flavours of the ingredients themselves. That was the secret.

If she made a dish of prawns fried in a wok with broccoli, she would add a few seasonings to it with an expert touch, and in the end it would just taste of prawns and broccoli.

To cook good Asian food, you have to understand seasoning. While Western cookery refers to seasoning mainly as the addition of salt, in Asian cuisines seasoning encompasses all five basic tastes, making sure they are all in balance in a dish.

THE FIVE BASIC TASTES

With so much variety in the world of food, it can be easy to forget that the way we taste is actually very simple. There are just five basic tastes that we perceive with our mouths – salty, sweet, sour, bitter and umami. The first four require very little explanation, but umami might be something new to you.

Outside of these five basic tastes, most of the other properties that we get from food are aromas sensed by our nose. The five basic tastes are fundamental to understanding Asian flavour and, as you'll see in the following pages, they can help us make sense of the sometimes confusing range of Asian seasoning products.

ALL ABOUT UMAMI

Umami originated as a Japanese term that can roughly translate to 'deliciousness'. It was scientifically identified in 1908 by Japanese chemist Kikunae Ikeda, but it has been understood in cooking for centuries, and was even referred to in the early nineteenth century as *osmazome* by the famous French gourmand Brillat-Savarin.

Umami is a broad savoury flavour that is also described as 'meaty' or 'brothy', and every cuisine in the world has managed to harness it in some form.

The taste of umami is produced from a reaction between a flavour molecule and a receptor on our tongues - the same way as salty, sweet, sour and bitter tastes are produced. The most common molecules that produce the umami taste are glutamate, inosinate, and guanylate. They are hugely important. These three molecules are found in high proportions in many of our most flavourful foods - aged cheeses, cured meats, dried mushrooms, fermented fish and vegetables, and even wine.

Umami has three properties that are particularly useful in cookery.

1   It can affect other tastes. The five basic tastes all affect each other to some extent (for example, salty tastes reduce our perception of bitterness), but with umami it is quite pronounced. In addition to its own savoury taste, umami enhances the saltiness and sweetness of foods, while reducing their sourness and bitterness.

2   Umami-rich ingredients can be combined to increase their effect. When different umami molecules are combined, the effect is greater than the sum of their parts. For example, when inosinate from chicken or beef bones is combined with glutamate from onion, carrot and celery, the result is a rich meaty flavour in many Western stocks, or when glutamate from kombu is combined with inosinate from dried bonito flakes, the result is a rich ichiban dashi, the cornerstone of many Japanese dishes. Many of the classic food combinations around the world can be explained by the relationships between umami-rich foods, and even dishes as simple as the Pork Belly, Cabbage and Shiitake Hotpot on page 13 can contain combinations of umami-rich ingredients.

3   Umami can be enhanced by cooking. Many preserving processes increase the umami content of foods, such as drying and fermentation. The umami content of mushrooms increases dramatically when they are dried. By far the most common method of increasing umami, however, is browning. Known as Maillard reactions (after Louis-Camille Maillard, the French scientist who described them first in 1912), these are reactions between amino acids and sugars that give cooked foods a brown appearance and produce new flavours. Maillard reactions explain why a well-seared steak tastes 'meatier' than raw beef and also explain the benefits of *wok hei* in wok cooking (see Lesson 4).

BRINGING IT ALL TOGETHER

In addition to the five basic tastes, Asian seasoning also includes alcohols and oils. These are used in much the same way as in Western cooking. Most aromatic and flavourful compounds are not soluble in water (essential oils, for example) and so their flavour must be extracted by oil or alcohol.

But by far the most crucial point to bear in mind is that these seasonings are not used as *flavourings*. Oyster sauce is not used to make a dish taste like oysters, nor fish sauce to make a dish taste like fish. These ingredients are used for one purpose, and it's the same purpose I searched for in my grandmother's cooking for years – to extract and enhance the natural flavours of the ingredients you choose.

SALTY/UMAMI

Soy sauces - Soy sauces are made from fermented soybeans and other grains. The varieties are nearly endless. Lighter soy sauces are lighter in both flavour and colour, and contain a higher proportion of grain to soybean. Combinations of light and dark soy sauces are common in Asian cooking. **1**

Fish sauces - Made from fermented fish, fish sauces are popular across Southeast Asia, where they form the base of many dishes in Thailand, Vietnam, Laos, Cambodia and the Philippines. There are even local fish sauces from Japan and China. **2**

Oyster sauce - Oyster sauce is a thick, sweet and savoury seasoning from Chinese cooking. Its sweetness makes it a popular general seasoning. **3**

Shrimp pastes - Shrimp pastes are made from dried and fermented shrimp, and can vary from soft pink pastes to very hard brown cakes. Of the shrimp pastes, the Malaysian *belacan* and Indonesian *terasi* are among the most well known. **4**

UMAMI AND MSG

One of the most controversial sources of umami is monosodium glutamate, or MSG, the naturally occurring sodium salt of glutamate sometimes sold as an additive to boost the umami in food. Despite being recognised as safe by food authorities around the world, some anecdotal accounts still report adverse effects after eating Asian food in the West, attributing those effects to added MSG. MSG is present in many foods, both natural and man-made, both Western and Asian, so if added MSG concerns you, just choose products that do not contain it. I avoid adding MSG not for any health concerns, but as a matter of taste. Umami must be balanced just like any other taste, and when adding MSG, the tendency is for dishes to be too strongly umami, which is just as unbalanced as a dish that is too salty, sweet, sour or bitter.

Miso - There are many types of misos used in Japanese cooking, differentiated by their composition. Soybean-only miso is dark, reddish and strongly flavoured, but misos with higher proportions of rice, barley, or other grains will be lighter in both flavour and colour. **5**

Korean chilli bean paste (*gochujang*) - This sweet and savoury paste of fermented chilli and soybean is a staple of Korean cooking. It is available in different strengths from mild heat to very spicy. **6**

Korean soybean paste (*doenjang*) - Similar to the chilli bean paste, *doenjang* is a style of Korean miso, made without chilli and a valuable source of umami in Korean cooking. **7**

Other fermented soybean products - Salted fermented black soybeans and fermented yellow beans are other fermented bean products used in Chinese cooking, and Chinese-influenced cooking around Asia. **8**

Kombu - Kombu is a type of kelp that is a main source of umami in Japanese cooking. It's commonly used to make stocks and pickles. It can be difficult to find in Australia. **9**

Bonito flakes - Bonito flakes or *katsuobushi* are shavings of dried bonito. They are used to make quick stocks such as the Bonito Stock on page 32, but also as a seasoning in cooking, or scattering over finished dishes. **10**

SWEET

Palm sugar - Palm sugar is the collective name given to sugars produced by crystallising the sap from any number of palm species. It can range in colour from light brown to a deep red-brown and can range in flavour from quite light (almost like white sugar) to a deep and earthy caramel. It is less sweet than white sugar and the two are often used together to get the right balance of flavour and sweetness. **1**

White sugar - Ordinary white sugar is very important to Asian cooking, as it provides sweetness without the other flavour properties of other sweeteners like palm sugar or *kecap manis*. **2**

Mirin - Mirin is a sweetened rice wine used in Japanese cooking. Although it serves the purpose of both an alcohol and a sweetener in cooking, it is mainly used for its sweetness. **3**

Kecap manis - *Kecap manis* is a strongly sweet-savoury sauce made from soybeans and caramelised sugar. While it could be technically classified as a soy sauce, the proportion of soybean is actually very low, and it is used more for its sweetness than its umami flavour. **4**

Korean corn syrup (*mul yut*) - Korean corn syrup is a mild-flavoured sweetener that is very commonly used as a source of sweetness in Korean cuisine. It's available from Asian grocers. **5**

SOUR

Rice vinegar - Rice vinegars are common all around Asia, but they form a key component of Japanese cuisine. Pure rice vinegar **6a** can be expensive, and so mild rice-flavoured grain vinegars **6b** have been increasing in popularity.

Citrus - Another popular sour seasoning in Southeast Asian cuisine is citrus juice. Lemons, limes and regional citrus like calamansi are all used for sourness and a mild citral flavour. Where a stronger citral flavour is needed, Asian cuisines often use lemongrass, or leaves from trees like kaffir lime. **7**

Tamarind - Tamarind is the pulp of the seed pod of the tamarind tree. Dissolved into a paste with water, it is used as a souring agent in many Southeast Asian cuisines. It can also be bought as a puree. **8**

Black vinegar - Black vinegar is a strongly flavoured umami and malty rice vinegar used in Chinese cooking. It's particularly good with dumplings. **9**

ALCOHOLS

Sake – Sake is the main alcohol used in Japanese cooking. A dry style of rice wine, sake was traditionally made from rice only, but now mild-flavoured cooking sakes are made with added alcohol. Cheap cooking sakes cost only a few dollars and are perfectly fine to use for cooking, but should not be used for drinking. **10**

Shaoxing wine – A staple of Chinese cooking, Shaoxing wine is made from fermented glutinous rice to produce a strongly flavoured cooking wine with a dry and malty flavour. Higher quality Shaoxing wines are made specifically for drinking. **11**

OILS

Vegetable oil – A neutrally flavoured vegetable oil is fine for most uses in Asian cookery. In Asian cooking, oil is flavoured by aromatic ingredients early in the cooking process (such as garlic), and then used to carry flavour around the dish. **12**

Peanut oil – For wok cooking, many people prefer peanut oil. The light nutty flavour of the oil assists with the formation of *wok hei* (see pages 74-75), although many commercially available peanut oils are so light in flavour as to be virtually indistinguishable from a neutral vegetable oil. **13**

Sesame oil – Sesame oil is a dark brown oil made from toasted sesame seeds and favoured for its strongly nutty flavour. Untoasted varieties are also used in Japanese and other cuisines, although much less frequently. **14**

Chilli oil – Chilli oil is a flavoured oil infused with the heat and flavour of chilli. It's used in many Asian dishes to provide both flavour and heat. **15**

SAUCES

Many sauces in Asian cuisines are used as condiments, in the same way you might offer salt, pepper or mustard at the table with a Western meal, or a wedge of lemon with fish. Served alongside other dishes, they help to season food as you eat it with a boost of saltiness, umami, sweetness, sourness, and perhaps a touch of chilli heat.

SAMBAL BELACAN

MAKES ½ CUP
PREPARATION TIME 10 MINS

In Bahasa Malay *sambal* is a general term for a sauce or paste, and this basic Malaysian condiment shows off the incredible umami power of the local fermented shrimp paste, or *belacan*.

INGREDIENTS
1 tbsp *belacan* (shrimp paste)
4 large red chillies, deseeded
2 bird's-eye chillies, deseeded
1 tbsp lime juice
½ tsp sugar

METHOD
1   Heat a small frypan over low heat and dry-fry the *belacan* on both sides until toasted, fragrant and easily crumbled.

2   Tear the chillies into smaller pieces and pound to a rough paste with a mortar and pestle.

3   Add the *belacan*, lime juice and sugar and pound to combine. Adjust seasoning to taste.

NUOC CHAM

MAKES 1 CUP
PREPARATION TIME 10 MINS

Many sauces from Southeast Asia feature a balance of savoury, sweet and sour. It's the basis of many popular Vietnamese and Thai dishes, and it's not hard to get right. It's simply a matter of balancing two tastes first, then adding a third. Follow the process in this recipe and you'll never go wrong.

INGREDIENTS
2 bird's-eye chillies
3 cloves garlic
¼ cup caster sugar
½ cup lime juice or lemon juice
½ cup fish sauce
Water, to dilute

METHOD
1   Pound the chillies and garlic with a mortar and pestle and add the caster sugar and lime juice. Taste and adjust the proportions of lime juice and sugar until it tastes balanced and pleasant.

2   Add the fish sauce a little at a time until the sauce tastes savoury. I prefer to store the sauce at this stage as it keeps longer. Dilute with water to taste when ready to use.

PATISMANSI

MAKES 4 TBSP
PREPARATION TIME 2 MINS

This Filipino sauce is used to provide a salty, umami and sour seasoning to many dishes.

INGREDIENTS
2 tbsp fish sauce
2 tbsp lime juice or lemon juice
A pinch sugar

METHOD
Combine ingredients in a small bowl.

NAM JIM JAEW

MAKES ⅔ CUP
PREPARATION TIME 5 MINS
COOKING TIME 5 MINS

This popular Thai dipping sauce for meats is far easier to make than it may first appear, and has a great balance of flavour, texture, spice and fragrance.

INGREDIENTS
½ tsp uncooked glutinous rice or other rice

1 tbsp tamarind pulp, loosened in ¼ cup hot water

2 tbsp fish sauce

1 tbsp caster sugar

2 tbsp lime juice

1 eschalot, minced

2 cloves garlic, peeled and minced

1 tsp chilli powder

1 bird's-eye chilli, finely sliced

2 tbsp shredded coriander

METHOD
1 Place the glutinous rice in a small frypan or saucepan and toast over medium heat until the rice appears chalky and lightly browned in spots. Grind to a coarse powder with a mortar and pestle. Mix the tamarind pulp with the ¼ cup hot water, working the mixture with your fingers or the back of a fork to loosen the seeds from the pulp. Pass the mixture through a sieve and discard the seeds, reserving the thick tamarind water.

2 Combine the rice, tamarind water and remaining ingredients in a small bowl and stir to combine.

PONZU

MAKES 1½ CUPS
PREPARATION TIME 5 MINS
COOKING TIME 5 MINS

This versatile citrus and soy-based sauce from Japan is more delicate than the pungent sauces of Southeast Asia.

INGREDIENTS
75ml sake

75ml mirin

¼ tsp caster sugar

150ml light soy sauce

75ml freshly squeezed lemon juice

METHOD
Bring the sake, mirin and sugar to a simmer in a small saucepan. Simmer for 1 minute, then add the soy sauce and return to a simmer. Remove from the heat and stir through the lemon juice.

CHILLIES IN SOY SAUCE

MAKES 1 SMALL DISH
PREPARATION TIME 2 MINS

In my family this simple condiment of chillies in soy sauce appears on the table every time we have a Chinese dinner. You can also add some garlic, a pinch of sugar, and/ or a squeeze of citrus if you like.

INGREDIENTS
2 bird's-eye chillies, thinly sliced

1 tbsp soy sauce

METHOD
Combine ingredients in a small bowl.

STOCKS

Stocks are the basis of good cooking in any cuisine, and if you want to produce good food you really need to know how to make them and use them. The great thing about Asian stocks is that they're generally simpler, faster and easier to make than their Western counterparts. Here are five great Asian stocks for home use, and some can even be made in as little as ten minutes.

COARSE STOCK

PREPARATION TIME 10 MINS
COOKING TIME 4 HOURS

A good multi-purpose stock such as this is a necessity in the Asian kitchen. Used instead of water, the umami of the stock will boost the flavour of anything you make with it, while also reducing kitchen waste. It's an excellent habit to get into.

INGREDIENTS
Offcuts of chicken or pork (meat, skin, bone), or a mixture
Offcuts of fragrant vegetables such as spring onion, onion, garlic and ginger
Offcuts of white vegetables such as daikon, winter melon and Chinese cabbage

METHOD
Add the ingredients to a large pot and cover with water. Bring to a very low simmer and simmer for around 4 hours. Strain and reserve the liquid.

SHIITAKE MUSHROOM STOCK

MAKES 1 LITRE
STANDING TIME 20 MINS

This vegetarian stock is full of umami. You can make it as a separate stock, or as part of many recipes when soaking the mushrooms and using the steeping liquid for cooking.

INGREDIENTS
5 dried shiitake mushrooms
1 litre water

METHOD
Rinse the dried mushrooms under running water very quickly to remove any dirt. Bring the water to the boil in a small saucepan then remove from the heat. Add the mushrooms and place a small plate or drop lid on top. Steep the mushrooms in the hot water for 20 minutes. Remove the mushrooms and keep them for another purpose.

BONITO STOCK

MAKES 750ML
PREPARATION TIME 2 MINS
COOKING TIME 5 MINS

Bonito flakes are made from fillets of bonito that are dried, fermented and smoked, then shaved very thinly. They have a delicious savoury flavour and make an excellent stock in just minutes.

INGREDIENTS
750ml water
20g bonito flakes

METHOD
Bring the water to a rolling boil in a small saucepan. Add the bonito flakes and boil for just a few seconds. Turn off the heat and allow the bonito flakes to sink to the bottom of the pot without stirring. Carefully skim any scum from the surface of the stock then strain the liquid through muslin.

ANCHOVY STOCK

MAKES 1½ LITRES
PREPARATION TIME 10 MINS
STANDING TIME 20 MINS
COOKING TIME 30 MINS

Dried fish are a great source of umami, which explains why anchovy stocks are popular in so many countries in Asia. Japanese, Korean and many Southeast Asian cuisines all include stocks from dried fish.

INGREDIENTS

1 cup dried anchovies

1½ litres cold water

1 onion, peeled (optional)

3 cloves garlic, peeled and bruised (optional)

3 slices ginger, peeled and bruised (optional)

METHOD

1   To avoid making the stock slightly bitter, pinch off the head and dark stomach section of each fish and discard, leaving the backbone and tail. Place the anchovies into 500ml of the water and set aside for 20 minutes.

2   Place the onion, garlic and ginger (if using) and the remaining water in a small saucepan over high heat. Bring to a simmer, reduce the heat and simmer for 15 minutes. Add the anchovies and the liquid they are soaking in and return to a simmer. Simmer for a further 10 minutes then strain the solids from the stock.

CHICKEN STOCK

MAKES ABOUT 1½ LITRES
PREPARATION TIME 5 MINS
COOKING TIME 4 HOURS

A good chicken stock is central to Chinese cooking. Large tins of powdered chicken stock are a common sight in many home kitchens (and restaurants, for that matter), but they really are not necessary. Chicken stock is so easy to make and so important - I make it every week.

INGREDIENTS

500g chicken bones

METHOD

1   Cover the chicken bones with cold water and bring to a vigorous boil. Empty the contents of the pot into a clean sink and rinse the bones and pot of any scum. Return the bones to the pot and cover the bones with water again. Bring to a low simmer over medium heat then reduce the heat to very low, partially cover and simmer over a very low heat (about 1 bubble breaking the surface every second) for about 4 hours.

2   The boiled bones can be reboiled for a lighter flavoured stock, or combined with additional ingredients such as spring onions, garlic and ginger for making a coarse stock.

1   **SHIITAKE MUSHROOM STOCK**
2   **CHICKEN STOCK**
3   **ANCHOVY STOCK**
4   **BONITO STOCK**
5   **COARSE STOCK**

4

5

CABBAGE AND SOYBEAN PASTE SOUP
Baechu doenjang guk

SERVES 4   PREPARATION TIME 10 MINS   **COOKING TIME 30 MINS**

This simple soup is classic Korean comfort food. It can be served either as a side dish, as part of a meal, or as the centrepiece of a meal itself.

INGREDIENTS

½ head Chinese cabbage

1 litre Anchovy Stock (page 33)

4 tbsp Korean soybean paste (*doenjang*)

¼ tsp salt

1 tsp Korean chilli powder (*gochugaru*), (optional)

METHOD

1   Trim the core from the cabbage, wash the leaves well and split in half vertically. Cut horizontally into 3cm pieces.

2   Place the Anchovy Stock, soybean paste, cabbage and salt in a large pot and bring to a simmer over medium heat. Add the chilli powder if using, reduce the heat to low and simmer, covered, for 20 minutes. Divide the soup between bowls to serve.

NOTES

An important difference between Japanese soybean paste (miso) and Korean soybean paste (*doenjang*) is that the Korean paste can be boiled without losing flavour or texture. Japanese miso should not be boiled.

This soup draws umami from both the soybean paste and the Chinese cabbage. Using umami-rich foods in combination improves the overall effect in flavour.

Serve a small bowl of this soup on its own or as an accompaniment to other dishes, or serve a large bowl with cooked short-grain rice and a few Banchan (pages 128-129) for a complete Korean meal. Add the rice to the soup and eat it as a kind of porridge.

MISO SOUP WITH SPINACH AND EGG
Horenso to tamago no miso shiru

SERVES 4 PREPARATION TIME 5 MINS **COOKING TIME 10 MINS**

This is a great beginner's miso soup that uses easily available ingredients. Miso soup can be served as an accompaniment with just about any Japanese meal. It's drunk directly from the bowl without the need for a spoon.

INGREDIENTS

100g spinach, washed

2 cups water

2 cups Bonito Stock (page 32), or 2 cups water

3-4 tbsp light-coloured miso paste, any kind, or a mixture

2 eggs

2 spring onions, trimmed and finely sliced

METHOD

1 Bring a large saucepan of water to the boil and add the spinach root-end first. After 10 seconds or so, plunge the leaves under the water and boil for a further minute. Remove from the water and plunge into cold water. Gently squeeze out as much water as possible, discard the roots and cut into 5cm lengths.

2 Bring the 2 cups of water and Bonito Stock to a simmer in another saucepan. Add the blanched spinach. Place the miso in a fine sieve or deep ladle and with a spoon dissolve the miso into the soup. Discard any undissolved solids left in the sieve or the base of the ladle. Do not let the soup return to the boil at any stage after adding the miso.

3 Crack the eggs into a small bowl and lightly beat with chopsticks. Stir them into the hot soup, keeping the pot on the heat for about 30 seconds so that the eggs don't cool the soup too much. The eggs should just set into wispy threads.

4 Place a teaspoon of spring onion slices in the bottom of a small bowl, ladle over the hot soup, and serve immediately.

NOTES

Miso soup can be made from any kind of miso, but I recommend using lighter coloured miso if you're just getting started. Lighter coloured misos will generally also be lighter in flavour than darker coloured misos. You can even mix misos together to create a unique soup flavour.

It's important to balance the amount of miso with the strength of the stock you are using. A stronger stock will need less miso, while soup made from water alone will need more.

This basic miso soup recipe can be used with many other ingredients. Sliced onion, clams, mushrooms, tofu and *wakame* (a kind of seaweed) are popular choices.

PORK SINIGANG

SERVES 6 PREPARATION TIME 15 MINS **COOKING TIME 1 HOUR**

The classic comfort foods of different countries can teach you a lot about their cuisines. The salty-sour flavour of this light Filipino tamarind stew is something many Filipinos grow up with.

INGREDIENTS

2 tbsp tamarind pulp, loosened in ½ cup hot water

1 tsp salt

1½kg pork belly, rib bones separated, meat cut into 5cm cubes

2 large tomatoes, cut into eighths

1 large onion, peeled and cut into eighths

4 tbsp fish sauce

2 medium potatoes, peeled and cut into 5cm chunks or 1 large taro root, peeled and cut into 5cm chunks

1 small eggplant, cut into 5cm chunks

3 large green chillies, stalks removed

1 cup okra, stalks removed

1 cup green beans, tails removed

1 bunch water spinach (*kang kong*), about 200g, washed and cut into 10cm lengths, or 3 heads bok choy, washed and quartered

Patismansi (page 28) and lemon wedges, to serve

METHOD

1   Mix the tamarind pulp with the ½ cup hot water, rubbing through with your fingers or a spoon to loosen the seeds from the pulp, pass through a sieve and discard the seeds, reserving the thick tamarind water.

2   Bring 2 litres of water to the boil in a very large pot. Add the salt, pork belly and ribs and return to the boil. Skim off any scum that rises to the surface. Add the tomatoes, onion, fish sauce, and tamarind water and simmer, covered, for 30 minutes.

3   Add the potatoes or taro and simmer for a further 10 minutes. Add the eggplant, chillies, okra and beans and simmer for 10 more minutes. Add the water spinach and simmer for 5 minutes, or until softened. Adjust the seasoning with some more fish sauce if needed. Serve with Patismansi and lemon wedges on the side.

NOTES

Filipino dishes tend to be less sweet than other Southeast Asian cuisines, but they still require a little sweetness for balance. In this case the sweetness comes from cooking onion, tomato, potato (or taro), and eggplant.

Understanding flavour means understanding your ingredients. Sweetness, sourness and savoury flavours don't only come from sugar, vinegar and salt – they are all found in various measures in the other ingredients you are using.

Tamarind is the fruit of the tamarind tree and it has a dominant sharp, sour flavour with just a little sweetness. It's the most popular souring agent for *sinigang*, although green mango, citrus or guava are also sometimes used.

KOREAN TOFU STEW
Sundubu jigae

SERVES 2 PREPARATION TIME 15 MINS **COOKING TIME 15 MINS**

Often cooked and served piping hot in the same ceramic bowl, this Korean stew has a lot going on. Mixing beef, prawns, squid, clams and vegetables might sound like a confusing combination, but building a umami-rich base means that it all works together perfectly.

INGREDIENTS

2 tbsp sesame oil

50g rump steak or pork belly, very thinly sliced

2 cloves garlic, peeled and minced

2 tbsp Korean chilli powder (*gochugaru*), or to taste

1½ tsp salt

½ small onion, peeled and finely chopped

4 medium spring onions, trimmed and cut into 5cm lengths, plus extra, thinly sliced, to serve

½ small zucchini, trimmed and cut into half moons

100g enoki mushrooms, ends trimmed and broken into clumps

1 litre Anchovy Stock (page 33)

6 raw prawns, peeled and deveined

50g squid, sliced into rings

12 clams

300g silken tofu, drained

1 egg

METHOD

1   Heat a small saucepan or claypot over medium heat and add the sesame oil. Fry the beef or pork until just browned, then add the garlic, chilli powder and salt and stir to coat the meat. Add the onion, spring onion, zucchini and mushrooms and stir for a further minute. Add the stock and bring to a simmer. Simmer for 5 minutes, then add the seafood. Return to a simmer and add the tofu, breaking it up into large pieces in the pot. Simmer for a further 5 minutes.

2   Remove the pot from the heat, immediately crack in an egg (or two) and stir through to thicken the stew. Scatter with spring onions and serve immediately.

NOTES

Although it may look spicy, mild versions of this stew can be made by using a milder Korean chilli powder. It has the same vibrant red colour but much less heat. Don't be tempted to substitute ordinary Western chilli powders as they tend to be too spicy and without as much chilli flavour.

Chilli should be used for flavour first and heat second. When mild enough, chilli heat can work like umami in enhancing flavours in the mouth, but too much heat can overpower everything.

Try a vegetarian version using mushrooms or *kimchi* in place of the meat and seafood.

PAD THAI

SERVES 2   PREPARATION TIME 15 MINS + 30 MINS SOAKING   COOKING TIME 10 MINS

It's a favourite in Thai restaurants in Australia but *pad thai* is no less popular in its native Thailand. Making a good *pad thai* comes down to two key points – a good balance of sweet, sour and savoury in the sauce, and noodles that remain separate and *al dente* in texture.

INGREDIENTS

180g dried thin, flat (rice stick) noodles

2 tbsp dried shrimp (optional)

2 tbsp vegetable oil

1 eschalot, peeled and minced

2 cloves garlic, peeled and minced

¼ tsp salt

8 raw prawns, peeled and deveined

80g very firm tofu, cut into 1cm cubes

1 cup Chinese chives, cut into 5cm lengths

½ tsp chilli powder, or to taste

1½ cups loosely packed beansprouts, plus extra to serve

2 tbsp crushed roasted peanuts, plus extra to serve

2 eggs

Lime or lemon wedges, to serve

Sauce

2 tbsp tamarind pulp, loosened in ½ cup hot water

1½ tbsp fish sauce

1 tbsp sugar

METHOD

1   Soak the noodles in plenty of cold water for at least 30 minutes, and soak the dried shrimp in hot water for at least 10 minutes.

2   For the sauce, mix the tamarind pulp with the hot water, rubbing through with your fingers or a spoon to loosen the seeds from the pulp, pass through a sieve and discard the seeds, reserving the thick tamarind water. Add the fish sauce and sugar, and stir to dissolve the sugar.

3   Heat a wok over medium-high heat and add the vegetable oil, minced eschalot, garlic, dried shrimp and salt, tossing until fragrant. Add the prawns, tofu, and Chinese chives and fry for about a minute. Remove the noodles from the water and shake off as much water as you can. A little water will still cling to the noodles which will help them soften as they cook. Add the noodles to the wok.

4   Add the sauce a little at a time, tossing it through the noodles and allowing it to be absorbed until the noodles soften but are still *al dente*.

5   Toss through the chilli powder, beansprouts and peanuts and toss for a minute, or until the beansprouts soften. Move all of the contents of the wok to one side and crack the eggs into the open side. Stir the eggs until they are just firm, then combine with the noodles.

6   Divide the *pad thai* between two plates and top with some extra beansprouts and peanuts. Serve with wedges of lime, and extra fish sauce, sugar and chilli powder to season.

NOTES

Some variations of *pad thai* add a bright-red roasted chilli or shrimp paste in oil, which are common in Thai cooking. These give the noodles a much redder colour.

LESSON 3
UNDERSTANDING TEXTURE

When it comes to the overall concept of taste, the texture of the food you make is at least as important as its flavour, if not more. This can be a difficult concept to get your head around at first, but trust me, it's quite true. There are any number of examples that bear it out.

The difference in taste between a crisp, fresh serving of Tempura (page 54) and a soggy, stale one has very little to do with flavour and an awful lot to do with texture. Perfectly cooked rice (page 100) is light and fluffy and worlds apart from the stodgy, waterlogged mess you get if you don't cook it right. I know which I'd prefer to eat. The difference between a steak at rare, medium and well done is more a comparison of texture than it is of flavour.

Even something as simple as taking a bit of meat and rice together in a single mouthful is an exercise in texture. Nobody looks at a piece of meat in a wok-fried dish and thinks it could do with a 'ricier' flavour, but yet we eat the two together to match the firm texture of the meat to the soft and fluffy texture of the rice.

TEXTURE IN ASIAN FOOD

More often than not, the textures we look for in Asian cuisines are not so different to what we might want in modern Western food. Meat should be meaty and tender, seafood firm and moist, and vegetables *al dente*, but not too soft.

One difference, however, is that where Western cuisines may cook various elements of a meal separately and bring them together on a plate to eat, Asian cuisines may seek to have a variety of textures combined in one dish as it's prepared.

A dish like Dragon and Phoenix (page 69) is defined by tender chicken, plump, springy prawns and crunchy snow peas, all tied together by a silky, almost slippery sauce thickened with cornflour.

In a Pork, Prawn and Green Papaya Salad (page 65), the combination and balance of textures is more important than even the balance of flavours, and every care taken with the fine knifework required will be repaid generously by the quality of the final dish.

The importance of texture to Asian food can also be illustrated by considering the variety of noodles in Asian cuisines. Asian noodles come in many shapes and sizes that affect their texture, but they are also cooked to differing levels depending on their variety and personal preference. Some are cooked quite *al dente*, like pasta, while others are cooked until they are soft and almost slimy. Even when ordering a bowl of ramen in Japan, you will often be asked how you want the noodles done, on a spectrum from firm (*katame*) to soft (*yarawakame*).

When attempting to cook any Asian dish, you have to think about more than just the flavour. Often the texture of the final dish will be the most important part of cooking, and texture is the sole responsibility of the cook. A dish that is lacking seasoning or balance in flavour can always be adjusted, even at the table, but one where the texture is wrong can rarely be salvaged.

Thankfully, creating texture in food is really quite simple. The texture of any dish will be the sum of the ingredients you choose, how you cut them, how you cook them, and how long you cook them for. Just keep those four factors in mind, and it's easy to control the texture of any dish.

1a   1b   1c   2a   2b   2c   3   4   5

Chinese cleavers – In classic Chinese cooking nearly all cutting is done with cleavers, and there are three main kinds. A lighter-weight slicer **1a** is used for most cutting of boneless meat and vegetables, a heel-weighted chopper **1b** is used for chopping meat, including bones, where contact is made closer to the heel or handle of the cleaver. Some cooks may prefer a toe-weighted cleaver **1c** for heavier work, as contact can be made with bones along the entire length of the cleaver.

Japanese knives – Japanese knives can be incredibly specialised, even down to types of knives being designed for individual species of fish. You don't need to worry about that level of speciality, as most Japanese knives are one of four main types. **An** *usuba hocho* or *nakiri bocho* **2a** is a thin, often rectangular knife used for cutting vegetables. The difference between the two is that the *usuba* is mainly for professional use and is only sharpened on an angle from one side, creating an off-centre point that allows for thinner and more delicate cuts than the *nakiri*, which is sharpened to a double-angled point like most Western knives. **A** *deba bocho* **2b** is a short, heavy knife used for filleting fish and sometimes poultry. Its weight is useful for cutting through fine bones and cartilage. **A** *yanagiba* **2c** is a long, thin knife for cutting sashimi. Its length allows the knife to be drawn through the fish in a single stroke, so as not to damage the delicate flesh with any sawing motions. **A** *santoku* (literally, 'three benefits') is an all-purpose knife that is used for meat, fish and vegetables, although Western style all-purpose knives known as *gyuto* (literally, 'beef knife') have increased in popularity as meat has become a larger part of the Japanese diet.

Multi-purpose knife – Outside of Japan and China, the rest of Asia tends to take a less prescriptive approach to knives. A cheap all-purpose knife is usually fine for most uses in a domestic kitchen, with a cleaver employed when heavy bones need to be cut. **3**

Mandoline – A mandoline is a very useful tool in the kitchen for fast and consistent thin slicing. Don't try and cut too much, though. The closer your fingers get to the blade the more dangerous it becomes. When using a mandoline, I cut the majority of slices of a vegetable on the mandoline, then finish each vegetable off with a knife to avoid accidents. **4**

Vietnamese shredder – These cheap shredding graters are perfect for quickly and consistently shredding vegetables like carrot, daikon (white radish), green papaya, and cucumber into thin strips for Vietnamese cooking. **5**

CHOOSING AND CARING FOR KNIVES

The simplest way to create texture in food is with a knife. Knowing how to use a knife well will save you time and money, and give you access to a whole range of different textures in your food.

Throughout my entire childhood my family had only a few knives for the kitchen. One was an old bone-handled English butter knife that my grandmother sharpened to a razor edge because she liked the quality of the steel. Another was a larger carbon steel knife that nobody quite knew where it came from, but which my grandmother kept sharp with the constant attention of a whetstone. The last was a big chopper that a blacksmith friend made for us. None of these knives cost more than a few dollars each, but they served us well for decades. My point is, a knife is only as good as you maintain it.

There is no point buying high-quality, expensive knives unless you plan to maintain them. Maintaining a knife means honing it often (at least once a week, but preferably every time you use the knife) to preserve the edge, and sharpening it when it needs it. For honing (removing tiny burrs and bends from the edge of the knife) and light sharpening, a honing steel or wheel sharpener is great, and you should keep one on hand in your kitchen at all times. For more comprehensive sharpening, you should use a whetstone, or have your knives professionally sharpened at least once a year.

KNIFE SKILLS

Cutting half-moons – For cylindrical vegetables, cut in half lengthways, then slice on an angle to produce half-moons.

Cutting shreds – For cylindrical vegetables, cut long, thin ovals on the diagonal and stack them in small piles. Thinly slice each pile into shreds or matchsticks. This is an Asian style of julienne.

Rolling cut – This cut produces irregular shapes of equal size. Cut through the vegetable on the diagonal. Roll the vegetable about one-third of a revolution and slice on the diagonal again. Repeat, rolling the vegetable back and forth to create irregular shapes. For large vegetables, you can halve or quarter them first.

Slicing meat for wok-frying – Starting at the left side of a thick steak (for right-handers), slice thin pieces with a sliding motion of the knife at an angle from right to left.

Slicing chicken for wok-frying – Take a chicken thigh fillet and divide it in half, just on the large side of the divide between the large lobe and small lobe. Slice each half into thick pieces with a slicing motion of the knife at an angle from right to left.

Slicing sashimi (square cut) – Starting at the right side of a piece of fish (for right-handers), make straight, even slices ½cm to 1½cm in width (depending on your preference) starting at the heel of the knife and drawing in a single stroke down to the point. Push each slice over to the right with the flat of the knife.

Slicing sashimi (angled cut) – Starting at the left side of a piece of fish, slice very thin pieces with a sliding motion of the knife at an angle from right to left. Place the slices in a line, and fold each piece over itself after each cut.

MIXED TEMPURA
Tempura no moriawase

SERVES 1–2 PREPARATION TIME 20 MINS **COOKING TIME 10 MINS**

Japanese cuisine has turned deep-frying into an art form. The goal for good tempura is a fine, light and crisp coating with a crunchy texture. It shouldn't taste oily.

INGREDIENTS

2 litres vegetable oil, for deep-frying

1 Japanese eggplant, sliced diagonally into 5mm slices

2 fresh shiitake mushrooms, caps only

2 asparagus spears

3 very large raw prawns, peeled and deveined, tails left intact

1 fillet garfish

Tempura batter

1 cup low-gluten (cake) flour, or plain flour mixed with 2 tbsp cornflour, plus extra for dusting

1 egg

1 cup cold water or soda water

5 ice cubes

Extra flour, for dusting

Tentsuyu

2 tbsp mirin

2 tsp caster sugar

1 cup Bonito Stock (page 32)

2 tbsp soy sauce

2 tbsp grated daikon, excess liquid squeezed out, to serve

1 tsp grated ginger (optional)

Green tea salt

1 tsp salt

¼ tsp powdered green tea (*matcha*)

METHOD

1   Sift the flour onto a tray and place, uncovered, in the freezer overnight.

2   For the *tentsuyu*, combine the ingredients in a small saucepan and bring to a simmer, stirring to dissolve the sugar. Allow to cool to room temperature. For the green tea salt, grind the salt and tea together with a mortar and pestle to a fine powder.

3   For the batter, whisk the egg and water together and add the ice cubes. Sift in the flour and stir with chopsticks to mix. Don't over-mix the batter (lumps are completely fine).

4   Lightly dust the vegetables in flour then draw them through the batter with chopsticks so that a very light coating clings to the outside.

5   Heat the oil in a wok or wide saucepan to 165°C. Slowly lower the vegetables into the oil, a few at a time, holding them for just a second to prevent them from sinking to the bottom of the pan. Fry for about 3–5 minutes, or until the vegetables are just tender. Drain on a wire rack.

6   Increase the heat of the oil to 175°C and repeat the frying process for the seafood, which should cook in about 3 minutes.

7   Serve the tempura with a small pile of green tea salt for dipping, and/or the *tentsuyu*, daikon and ginger. Mix the daikon and ginger with the *tentsuyu* just before eating.

NOTES

The secret to a crispy tempura batter is reducing the development of gluten. Gluten is fantastic for bread and noodles, but not great for crispy batter. Freezing the flour in this recipe keeps it dry and cold, stopping the gluten from developing.

Drying the tempura on a wire rack rather than paper allows air to circulate around it, carrying away steam that would otherwise make it soggy.

MIXED SASHIMI
Sashimi moriawase

SERVES 2 PREPARATION TIME 15 MINS **STANDING TIME 10 MINS + 15 MINUTES COOLING**

Sashimi is a perfect example of how important texture is to taste. Just a few simple strokes of a knife can turn a big hunk of raw fish into a delicate, refined and delicious meal. Sashimi calls for a lighter but umami-rich soy sauce to accentuate the natural umami in the fish without overpowering its flavour. Many commercial soy sauces are too heavy to match with sashimi or even sushi, so this *tosa joyu* is a good seasoning to have on hand.

INGREDIENTS

100g sashimi-grade tuna, skin removed

100g sashimi-grade salmon, skin and bones removed

100g sashimi-grade snapper, skin and bones removed

Very finely shredded daikon radish, to serve

Perilla (*shiso*) leaves, to serve

Wasabi, to serve

Tosa joyu

2 tbsp sake

2 tbsp mirin

200ml soy sauce

1 piece kombu (optional)

A handful bonito flakes

METHOD

1   Slice the fish as shown on page 53.

2   For the Tosa Joyu, bring the sake and mirin to a simmer and simmer for 1 minute. Add the soy sauce and kombu, if using, and bring to a simmer again, removing the kombu before bubbles appear. Add the bonito flakes and remove from the heat. Allow to stand for 10 minutes then strain and allow to cool.

3   To serve, place a mound of shredded daikon on a plate and add the fish and *shiso* leaf in front of it. Place a small mound of wasabi on the plate and serve with the Tosa Joyu for dipping.

NOTES

Sashimi is always served with edible garnishes known as *tsuma* or *ken*. They are very important both visually and for flavour, as you can munch on them as a palate cleanser. In this case I've suggested shredded daikon and *shiso* leaf, but you could use finely shredded cucumber or carrot, or a mound of *wakame* (a type of seaweed).

It is also important to serve *karami* (any kind of spicy condiment) with sashimi. Most common is wasabi, but you could also use grated ginger, garlic or even hot mustard or chilli. Ginger is particularly common with oily fish such as mackerel.

CHICKEN AND VEGETABLE NIMONO
Tori to yasai no nimono

SERVES 4 PREPARATION TIME 15 MINS + 20 MINS SOAKING **COOKING TIME 20 MINS**

Even in a simple stew, how you cut the meat and vegetables has a huge impact on the texture and taste of the dish. If all the vegetables in this home-style Japanese recipe were cut into small cubes the dish would be boring and homogenous, but with each of the mushrooms, carrot, daikon and onion in their own shape, every element has its individual character.

INGREDIENTS

12 dried shiitake mushrooms

1 tsp vegetable oil

500g chicken thighs, skin and bone removed, cut into 2cm strips

1 daikon, peeled and cut into 3cm rounds, edges bevelled

2 small carrots, peeled and cut into 5cm chunks

6 large spring onions, trimmed, and white and light green part cut on an angle into 5cm lengths, dark green part finely sliced

1 tbsp caster sugar

1 tbsp sake

2 tbsp mirin

2 tbsp soy sauce

METHOD

1 Rinse the shiitake mushrooms under running water and steep them in 1 litre of hot water for 20 minutes. Drain the mushrooms, reserving the liquid, then remove and discard the stalks and halve the caps on an angle.

2 Heat the oil in a large saucepan over high heat and fry the chicken until lightly browned. Add the daikon, carrot, shiitake mushroom caps and the white and light green parts of the spring onion, stirring for 5 minutes, or until the vegetables start to soften. Add in enough of the shiitake soaking liquid to just cover the chicken and vegetables and bring to a simmer.

3 Stir in the sugar, sake, mirin and soy sauce and cover the pot with a drop lid or cartouche (see below). Simmer over low heat for 15–20 minutes, or until the vegetables are tender. Allow the chicken and vegetables to cool in the liquid, then reheat to serve.

4 Put the chicken and vegetables in a bowl and pour over just a little of the simmering liquid, then serve scattered with the finely sliced spring onion tops.

NOTES

Nimono is Japanese for a stew or simmered dish, and it's a staple in every Japanese household. Try it with beef, pork, seafood or just keep it vegetarian.

Japanese cuisine often uses drop-lids; round wooden lids that fit inside the pot, holding ingredients below the surface of a simmering liquid. A small circle of baking paper, or a crumpled piece of aluminium foil works just as well.

DRESSED CUCUMBER
Kyuuri no sunomono

MAKES 1 SERVING FOR SHARING PREPARATION TIME 20 MINS

Taking a bit of care with the way you cut even a single vegetable can make or break a dish. This cutting style looks impressive but is actually very easy, and it creates a delicious texture in the cucumber.

INGREDIENTS

2 Lebanese cucumbers

1 tbsp salt

1 tbsp Bonito Stock (page 32), or water

1 tbsp rice vinegar

1 tsp sugar

½ tsp soy sauce

METHOD

1   Peel a few strips of skin from the cucumber (don't peel completely). Slice the cucumber diagonally two-thirds of the way through in slices 1 millimetre apart. Roll the cucumber over so that the cuts are facing the board and repeat for the other side of the cucumber. If you cut on the same angle the cuts on each side will be perpendicular to one another and the cucumber will not be divided.

2   Mix the salt with 2 cups cold water and soak the cut cucumbers in the water for at least 10 minutes, until the cucumbers soften. Carefully squeeze out as much liquid as possible and cut the cucumbers into 4cm lengths.

3   Mix the stock, vinegar, sugar and soy sauce together until the sugar is dissolved. Place the cucumber in a serving bowl and pour over the dressing. Serve immediately.

NOTES

Pickles and vinegared dishes are popular in Japanese cuisine as sour and sometimes sweet accompaniments to balance strongly savoury dishes.

This is delicious served with Salt-grilled Salmon (page 155), rice, and some Miso Soup (page 38).

With their thinner skins and fewer seeds, Japanese cucumbers are a different variety to Lebanese cucumbers. If using the Japanese ones you don't need to peel them.

POPCORN CHICKEN WITH BASIL
Yan su ji

SERVES 2-4 PREPARATION TIME 20 MINS **COOKING TIME 10 MINS**

Taiwanese food is a great mix of local dishes with influences from China, Japan and Southeast Asia. Popcorn chicken is a popular street food in Taipei, and once you try it you'll see why. The crunchy texture of the sweet potato flour coating is incredible.

INGREDIENTS

600g boneless chicken thigh fillets, preferably skin-on, cut into 3cm pieces

3 cloves garlic, peeled and minced

1 tsp grated ginger

1 tbsp soy sauce

1 tbsp Shaoxing wine

2 tsp sugar

½ tsp Chinese five spice powder

1 cup sweet potato flour

2 litres oil, for deep-frying

1 cup loosely packed Thai basil leaves

Spice salt

1 tbsp salt

¼ tsp Chinese five spice powder

¼ tsp white pepper

A pinch chilli powder

METHOD

1 Combine the chicken with the garlic, ginger, soy sauce, Shaoxing wine, sugar and five spice powder and set aside to marinate for at least 10 minutes.

2 Coat the chicken pieces in the sweet potato flour and shake off any excess.

3 Heat the oil in a wok or saucepan. When the oil reaches 150°C scatter the basil leaves into the wok and stir for about 20 seconds, or until the basil turns translucent. Remove the basil from the wok and drain on absorbent paper.

4 Increase the heat of the oil to 170°C and fry the chicken in batches for about 3 minutes, or until golden brown and cooked through, regularly skimming any floating flour bits from the oil.

5 For the spiced salt, mix the ingredients together and toast in a dry frypan over low-medium heat for 2 minutes, or until fragrant. Toss the chicken with the fried basil leaves and season with a good pinch of the spice salt. Serve immediately.

NOTES

Sweet potato flour is sometimes sold as 'tapioca flour'. It's available from Asian grocers. The Taiwanese variety is a coarse-textured but light flour that gives the characteristic crumbly texture to this dish. You could substitute cornflour or rice flour but it won't quite be the same.

When deep-frying, skimming oil is a really important step that many people overlook. It preserves the oil by keeping it clear, and stops burnt flavours creeping in to later batches.

PORK, PRAWN AND GREEN PAPAYA SALAD
Goi du du tom thit

SERVES 2 PREPARATION TIME 25 MINS **COOKING TIME 10 MINS**

Green papaya salads are found throughout Southeast Asia. In the Thai and Laos versions, *som tam* and *tam mak hoong*, everything is lightly pounded in a mortar and pestle to mix the juices with the dressing. Vietnam has two popular versions: one with basil and dried beef in a soy sauce dressing, and this one from the south – a riot of flavours and textures that's surprisingly easy to make.

INGREDIENTS

150g pork belly, skin and bone removed

6 large raw prawns, peeled and deveined

300g green papaya, peeled and very finely shredded (substitute green mango or 2 continental cucumbers, seeds discarded)

1 small carrot, peeled and very finely shredded

½ cup Nuoc Cham (page 28)

½ cup loosely packed torn Vietnamese mint or mint leaves

½ cup loosely packed torn coriander leaves

½ cup loosely packed torn Asian basil leaves

¼ cup roasted peanuts

¼ cup fried eschalots (see below)

METHOD

1 Place the pork in a small saucepan and cover with cold water. Bring to a simmer, skim off any scum and simmer for 5 minutes. Add the prawns and simmer for a further 3–4 minutes, or until the prawns are cooked through. Remove the pork and prawns from the liquid, rest for 5 minutes then slice the pork thinly and the prawns in half along their length.

2 Toss the papaya and carrot with half of the Nuoc Cham and set aside in the fridge for 5 minutes. If using cucumber you can skip this step.

3 Toss the pork and prawns with the papaya, carrot and fresh herbs then dress with the remaining Nuoc Cham. Lightly crush the peanuts with a mortar and pestle and scatter over the salad. Scatter the fried eschalots over the salad and serve.

NOTES

Raw green papaya has a fresh, tangy taste and crisp texture which is very different from ripe papaya, but it isn't available year-round. Cucumber is a great substitute. I actually make this recipe with cucumber far more often than I do with papaya!

Crispy fried eschalots are available in containers from Asian grocery stores often labelled as 'fried onion'. This salad would be nothing without its textures. The green papaya or cucumber form the base texture, the pork gives a meaty bite, the prawns a springy bounce, then there's lightness from the herbs, and a final, satisfying crunch from the peanuts and fried eschalots.

CHICKEN AND COCONUT CURRY NOODLES
Khao soi

SERVES 4 PREPARATION TIME 30 MINS **COOKING TIME 30 MINS**

From the sweet, creamy soup freshened with plenty of lime, to the two different textures of noodle, this Northern Thai dish is a fantastic example of balance both in flavour and texture.

INGREDIENTS

¼ cup vegetable oil, plus extra for deep-frying

4 boneless chicken thigh fillets

¼ cup fish sauce, plus extra, to serve

2 tbsp soy sauce

2 tbsp (50g) chopped palm sugar

1 cup chicken stock or water

2 cans (800g) coconut milk

2 tbsp lime juice

1kg fresh egg noodles

Curry paste

1 brown onion or 4 eschalots

3 large dried chillies, soaked in hot water for 10 minutes

1 lemongrass stalk, tender core only

5cm ginger, peeled

2 coriander roots, root and thick stalks only (leaves and thin stalks reserved for serving)

4 cloves garlic, peeled

1 tsp curry powder

1 tsp coriander powder

1 tsp turmeric powder

1 tsp *belacan* (shrimp paste)

METHOD

1   Blend the curry paste ingredients in a food processor to a smooth paste.

2   Heat a medium saucepan over medium heat, add ¼ cup oil, then the curry paste and fry for about 5 minutes, stirring until the paste is very fragrant. Add the chicken, fish sauce and soy sauce and fry for 5 minutes, turning the chicken regularly and stirring so that the paste does not catch. Add the palm sugar and chicken stock, bring to a simmer and simmer for a further 5 minutes. Add the coconut milk and return to a simmer, then turn off the heat. Remove the chicken from the soup and tear it into rough strips with two forks. Return the chicken to the soup, stir through the lime juice, taste and adjust for seasoning.

3   Heat about 2 cups of oil in a separate saucepan to 170°C and fry 200g of the egg noodles for about 4 minutes, or until crisp, then drain. Boil the remaining noodles in water according to the packet directions.

4   To serve, divide the boiled noodles between four large bowls and add ladles of soup and chicken, leaving lots of room in the bowl for the condiments. Serve along with the condiments in small bowls or plates on the table.

Condiments, to serve

1 cup sliced eschalots

Coriander leaves (see curry paste ingredients)

Small bowls of fish sauce, chilli powder and sugar

Lime wedges

2 cups pickled mustard greens, roughly chopped

NOTES

The soup is deliberately under-seasoned; condiments are put on the table so everyone can season the dish to their taste.

DRAGON AND PHOENIX

SERVES 2, OR MORE IF SHARED PREPARATION TIME 20 MINS **COOKING TIME 10 MINS**

One of the most important textures in Asian cooking is silkiness. It's a texture found in Japanese seaweed dishes and Chinese soups and sauces, but probably the most familiar expression is in classic Cantonese stir-fried dishes. Done badly, silky sauces can be thick and gluggy, but done well they are a luxurious pleasure.

INGREDIENTS

6 raw prawns, peeled and deveined

2 chicken thigh fillets, cut into small medallions (see page 52)

½ cup vegetable oil

4 spring onions, trimmed and cut into 5cm lengths

½ small carrot, peeled, halved lengthways and sliced diagonally into thin crescents

1 cup snow peas, trimmed

5 slices ginger, bruised

Sauce

1 tbsp Shaoxing wine

½ cup Coarse Stock (page 32), Chicken Stock (page 33) or water

¼ tsp salt

½ tsp sugar

½ tsp cornflour

Marinade

1 egg white

1 tsp cornflour

¼ tsp salt

2 tsp Shaoxing wine

METHOD

1   Butterfly the prawns by cutting the back lengthways almost completely through. Press down into the cut with the flat of your knife to flatten the prawn. Mix the prawns and chicken with the marinade ingredients. Set aside for at least 15 minutes.

2   Heat about 2 cups of water in the wok until boiling and add 1 tbsp of the oil. Blanch the spring onions and carrots for about 2 minutes, adding the snow peas in the final minute, until the vegetables are slightly softened. Remove the vegetables, discard the water and dry the wok over the flame.

3   Add the remaining oil to the hot wok then add the ginger, fry the chicken and prawns (in batches if necessary), tossing for about 3-4 minutes or until they are cooked through. Remove from the wok and discard the oil.

4   Combine the sauce ingredients and add to the wok, bring to the boil, then toss the chicken, prawns and vegetables through the sauce until it thickens. Remove to a plate and serve.

NOTES

The key to a silky sauce is the right proportions of oil, liquid and thickener (in this case, cornflour). Too much oil and the sauce will be too rich, too much thickener and it will be too heavy, and too much liquid and it will be insipid.

Keep in mind that the sauce will thicken further as the dish begins to cool out of the wok, so leave the sauce a little thin at the end of cooking to allow for this.

There is a lot of symbolism in Asian cooking, particularly around celebratory times. This Cantonese dish is served around Chinese New Year; the prawns represent a dragon and the chicken represents a phoenix – two auspicious mythical animals in Chinese culture.

LESSON 4
THE WOK

Woks are fundamental to Asian cooking, so it's worth getting to know your way around one. They originated in China, where they're still the main pot used in the kitchen, but these days you'll also find woks throughout Southeast Asia, Japan and even India.

They're mostly used for fast frying and tossing ingredients over high heat (what we would call 'stir-frying' in English), but the true charm of a wok is in its versatility: you can use them for boiling, braising, deep-frying, shallow-frying and even steaming.

In this lesson we'll go through the best technique for wok-frying from the most basic wok-fried dishes to some that are a little more challenging, and learn how to create the essence of wok-fried flavour – *wok hei*.

CHOOSING A WOK

Size

When choosing the size of your wok don't think about how much food you want to cook, think about the size of flame you're going to put it on. The bigger and stronger the flame, the bigger the wok you can handle. While woks used over large commercial burners can be around 50 centimetres in diameter, for home use a wok around 35 centimetres in diameter is a good choice, even over the very largest of domestic burners. Even if you're only cooking for one, the wok's curved shape allows very small amounts of food to be cooked even in the largest of woks.

Material

Woks are generally made of cast iron, carbon steel, stainless steel or aluminium and are very thin at only around 2–3 millimetres in thickness. My choice is carbon steel.

When very thin, cast iron can be brittle and crack if not handled with care. Stainless steel can lose its seasoning quickly. Aluminium is soft and can easily dent and deform, and is reactive to acidic foods. Carbon steel is durable and easy to care for.

I avoid non-stick woks as they are often designed for medium heat rather than the high temperatures of wok cooking. They also tend to be thick and heavy, giving less control over heat zones. And nothing sticks to a well-seasoned wok when used correctly.

Handles

Woks may have a single wooden stick handle 1, protruding from the wok like the handle of an ordinary frypan, or double loop handles 2 on opposite sides of the wok. Loop handles are metal, will get hot during cooking, and must be held with a folded damp cloth.

For domestic-sized woks I find the stick handles most useful, as the wok can be tossed in the same manner as a frypan. On larger commercial woks, long stick handles are less effective and can be dangerous, and so I prefer loop handles.

Base

Woks have either a curved or flat base. A curved base is more traditional and easier to cook with, but needs a wok ring or trivet to keep it steady during cooking. A flat-based wok gives less control over heat and liquid, but it can be placed directly on a flat gas stove.

For flat electric or induction stoves, flat-bottomed woks can be used but their small point of contact means that only a small amount of heat is transferred. On these stoves my advice is to avoid woks altogether. Excellent results can be achieved in a large, good-quality frypan.

SEASONING A WOK

Seasoning a wok is a process of burning thin layers of oil onto the surface of the metal, making the wok easier to use and protecting it from corrosion. Scientifically, the process is called 'polymerisation' – in the presence of the iron of the wok, oil molecules oxidise to a hard, non-stick surface. To season a wok is simple, and all you need is a wok, a roll of paper towel and a bit of vegetable oil.

1   Wash the wok in warm soapy water and rinse it thoroughly. Dry the wok well.

2   With paper towel, wipe a very thin layer of oil all over the inside of the wok, removing any excess with clean paper towel. If you use too much oil, it will not oxidise well and will become sticky.

3   Heat the wok over medium heat for about 10 minutes. It may smoke quite a lot so open your doors and windows.

4   Rotate the wok over the heat so that it heats evenly.

5   Remove the pan from the heat and wipe away any burned oil with a clean paper towel.

6   Repeat steps 2–5 at least three times until the wok takes on a dull black appearance.

WOK EQUIPMENT

Wok brush. Rather than completely washing a wok between dishes, it can be brushed under running water to remove any food, then returned to the heat to dry. Any stiff, natural-fibre kitchen brush will do. Beware of plastic bristles as they can melt when used with a hot wok. **1**

Spider. This long-handled sieve is perfect for removing ingredients that have been blanched or fried. **2**

Wok spatula. A wok spatula is a long-handled metal spatula used for moving ingredients in a wok. Its familiar shape makes it a great tool for getting started with wok cooking. **3**

Wok ladle. A wok ladle is a truly versatile tool. Its round bowl is used to reach and measure ingredients or seasonings, to scoop water or oil, and for cooking. It's my preferred tool for wok cooking, but can take some getting used to. **4**

Wok ring or trivet. Either of these will keep a round-bottomed wok steady when cooking on a gas stove. **5**

CLEANING AND MAINTENANCE

Clean your wok straight after using it by brushing out any solids and excess oil with a stiff brush under running water while the wok is still hot. Return the wok over heat to dry it completely and burn away any residue. You don't need to use detergents, as heating the wok will kill bacteria and burn away excess oil.

Just brushing and heating the wok should keep it in good working order, but every few months I like to add a layer or two of seasoning to keep my wok performing at its best.

WOK TECHNIQUE

Some call it 'stir-frying' but the technique of frying in a wok involves almost no stirring at all. Wok-frying is more about moving the wok and using its curved shape to toss ingredients, and the goal of good wok technique is to achieve that characteristic wok-fried flavour known in Cantonese as *wok hei*. A curved ladle or flat spatula are often used, but most of the motion is caused by tossing the wok itself, with the tools just used to keep control.

Wok hei (also called *wok qi* in certain dialects) translates as the 'spirit' or 'breath' of the wok, but it isn't as mystical as the name may suggest. *Wok hei* refers to the slightly smoky, slightly umami taste of food that has been fried over high, dry heat.

When cooking with your wok at home, you don't need to copy the theatrics of Chinese chefs in commercial kitchens, tossing woks at speed with a clatter of metal and ingredients flying in constant motion. In fact, if you do so, you probably won't get the result you're after.

The heat output of a commercial wok burner is four or five times greater than the stovetop wok burners we use at home. Heat that high will brown meat, caramelise sugars and vaporise liquids in seconds for perfect *wok hei*, but in a domestic kitchen we need to take a slightly different approach to get it right.

The way to achieve great *wok hei* at home is firstly – and most importantly – *never overcrowd the wok*. Meat, seafood and vegetables all give off liquid when they are cooked, and in an overcrowded wok that liquid will not evaporate quickly enough. The ingredients will steam and stew instead of frying. Fry individual ingredients in small batches if you need to, combining everything at the end for a complete dish.

Remember also that you don't need to toss the ingredients constantly. Tossing the wok stops ingredients from burning in contact with the wok. This is very important against the heat of commercial woks, but at home the challenge is the opposite. You want ingredients to brown and slightly char for your *wok hei*. Pieces of meat will brown faster if spread out in a single layer for as much contact with the wok metal as possible and left there for a while rather than fussing over them and prodding and poking at them. Only toss the wok when you need to.

Don't add liquids too early in the process. Many of the seasonings used in wok cooking are in liquid form, so it's often best to fry other ingredients first, then add liquid seasonings towards the end of cooking.

COMPOSING A WOK-FRIED DISH

When cooking a wok-fried dish, the key is to keep it simple.

Around Asia, most wok-fried dishes will use just a few ingredients, maybe just one meat or seafood cooked on its own, or perhaps combined with no more than one or two vegetables and a few light seasonings. Certainly the Western style 'stir-fries' containing one kind of meat and up to a dozen different mixed vegetables slathered in thick, overpowering sauces are rarely found in Asian home cooking.

A good analogy is to think of composing a wok-fried dish like mixing coloured paints, with each ingredient as a colour. The aim is to create something simple and clean by using colours that work together. The more colours you use, the more complicated and confused the mixture becomes, and ultimately when you mix too many colours together, everything turns out the same shade of brown.

A wok-fried dish should taste of its ingredients, and not of the seasonings added into it. A light hand with selecting ingredients, as well as with adding seasonings, will produce a dish that is light and full of natural flavour.

Texture, too, is very important. Avoid the thick 'stir-fry strips' in the supermarket and cut your ingredients yourself. Examples for cutting meat and poultry for the wok are on page 52, and on the facing page there are some ideas for cutting vegetables in shapes that also suit wok cooking.

EGG FRIED RICE

SERVES 2 PREPARATION TIME 5 MINS **COOKING TIME 5 MINS**

This basic fried rice is a good choice for your first attempt at wok-frying. No meat or delicate vegetables to worry about – just a simple dish that will work well with good wok technique.

INGREDIENTS

3 eggs

1 tsp sesame oil

¾ tsp salt

2 tbsp vegetable oil

3 spring onions, white and light green parts finely sliced

2 cloves garlic, peeled and minced

4 cups leftover cooked jasmine rice, cold

1 tbsp soy sauce

¼ tsp white pepper

METHOD

1   Beat the eggs with the sesame oil and ¼ tsp of salt and set aside. Heat the wok over medium-high heat and add the vegetable oil. Add half the spring onions, garlic and the remaining salt and fry until fragrant. Add the rice and soy sauce and toss to coat in the oil, pressing the rice against the side of the wok to break up any clumps.

2   When the rice softens and begins to toast, move all the rice to one side of the wok and add the egg mixture to the open side. Stir the eggs until they are nearly set, then combine with the rice. Add the remaining spring onions and white pepper and toss through.

NOTES

Oil is very important to wok cooking. To carry flavour around any wok-fried dish, you must flavour the oil first. Adding half the spring onions with the garlic will flavour the oil to form the base of the dish. The remainder added at the end provide a fresh flavour and texture.

Fried rice is easiest when made with leftover rice that has been cooked and refrigerated. The refrigerated rice is firmer and will soften as it reheats in the wok. You can use freshly cooked rice but you need to use a lighter touch in the wok to keep from mashing it. The rice needs to lightly toast to give the dish a good *wok hei* taste.

Once you've mastered the technique of making basic fried rice, you can start adding other ingredients. Add meat and vegetables, use up leftovers, or just move on to the Nasi Goreng Ayam recipe on page 123.

STIR-FRIED BEANSPROUTS WITH GARLIC

MAKES 1 SERVING PREPARATION TIME 5 MINS **COOKING TIME 5 MINS**

Before we move on to frying meat in a wok, this simple vegetable dish is an example of how to handle one of the most common issues arising when wok-frying – dealing with liquid.

INGREDIENTS

2 tbsp vegetable oil

3 cloves garlic, peeled and finely chopped

¼ tsp salt

1 small carrot, peeled and finely shredded

1 small green capsicum, deseeded and finely sliced

2 cups beansprouts

1 tbsp soy sauce

1 tbsp Shaoxing wine

½ tsp sesame oil

½ tsp cornflour mixed with 1 tbsp cold water or stock

White or black pepper, to serve

METHOD

1   Heat a wok over high heat and when smoking, add the vegetable oil. Add the garlic and salt and quickly stir the garlic through the oil until it is fragrant. This will only take a few seconds. Add the carrot and capsicum and toss for about a minute, or until the vegetables begin to soften and release their moisture.

2   Add the beansprouts, soy sauce, Shaoxing wine, and sesame oil and toss for a further minute, or until the beansprouts soften. Drizzle in the cornflour mixture slowly while constantly tossing the wok to thicken the sauce. Sprinkle with pepper to serve.

NOTES

Keep the wok heat very high. All the ingredients cook quickly, so the high heat will evaporate as much liquid as possible in a short time.

The liquid released from the vegetables is both a blessing and a curse. It contains a lot of flavour, but it also makes it more difficult to achieve good *wok hei.*

Drizzling the cornflour mixture into the wok slowly rather than dumping it all in at once will thicken the liquid evenly, allowing it to coat the vegetables without clumping.

BEEF AND BASIL
Nua pad krapow

SERVES 2 PREPARATION TIME 10 MINS **COOKING TIME 15 MINS**

This is the one dish I always recommend people to start out with when cooking with their wok, as it illustrates all the most important points of wok cooking – texture, volume, versatility and balancing seasonings. Best of all, it's forgiving. If you don't get it exactly perfect, it's still going to taste great.

INGREDIENTS

250g rump or chuck steak, or 250g
   beef mince

3 garlic cloves, peeled

1 large red chilli (mild), or 2 bird's-eye
   chillies (hot), or a combination

2 tbsp peanut oil

1 tsp sugar

2 tbsp fish sauce

1 cup loosely packed Asian basil leaves
   (holy basil preferable, but any basil
   is fine)

Crisp fried eggs

½ cup peanut oil

2 eggs

METHOD

1 If using steak, roughly mince with a heavy knife or cleaver and transfer to a bowl. Place the garlic and chillies on a chopping board and roughly chop them together.

2 Heat a wok over very high heat and when smoking, add the peanut oil around the edges of the wok so it drips down to the base of the wok. Add the chopped chillies and garlic and stir in the oil until fragrant.

3 Add the beef and sugar and toss for a minute until the sugar starts to caramelise and the beef browns. Toss through the fish sauce and let the beef simmer for just a minute. Taste the beef and adjust seasoning.

4 Toss through the basil until it just wilts, then empty the contents of the wok to a separate bowl. Brush out the wok under running water and return it to the heat to dry.

5 When the wok is dry and hot, add the oil for the eggs. Crack in one egg and slowly spoon a few ladles of oil over the egg. Continue ladling over the oil until the edges of the egg crisp, and the white sets over the yolk. Repeat for the remaining egg. Serve the beef over the rice, topped with an egg.

NOTES

If you're new to wok cooking, perhaps start by making this with mince. Once you're a bit more confident you can try chopping the meat yourself. The difference in texture is worth the extra effort.

If the beef releases a lot of liquid, it's best to keep cooking it until the liquid evaporates and concentrates the flavour.

LEMONGRASS BEEF
Thit bo xao sa ot

SERVES 4 PREPARATION TIME 10 MINS **COOKING TIME 10 MINS**

Frying meat in a wok is easy, provided you follow three simple rules – cut the meat thinly, brown it well and, of course, the cardinal rule, never overcrowd the wok. This is one of my favourite Vietnamese dishes and because there are no vegetables to worry about, you can just focus on getting the flavour of the wok-cooked meat just right.

INGREDIENTS

¼ cup peanut oil

500g rump steak, sirloin or flank, very thinly sliced

1 small brown onion, peeled and sliced

2 stalks lemongrass, tender white part only, minced

3 cloves garlic, peeled and minced

1 large red chilli, sliced diagonally

2 tbsp fish sauce

1½ tsp sugar

¼ tsp freshly ground black pepper

METHOD

1   Heat a wok over very high heat until smoking, add half the oil and fry the beef in batches until well browned all over then remove from the wok.

2   Add the remaining oil to the wok and fry the onion, lemongrass, garlic and chilli until the onions are softened and the ingredients are fragrant and starting to brown. Return the beef to the wok and toss with the fish sauce, sugar and black pepper for about 2 minutes. Remove from the wok and allow to rest for a minute before serving.

NOTES

If you use the woody parts of the lemongrass or don't cut it into small enough pieces, the dish will have a gritty texture. If the lemongrass is especially woody, whizz it in a food processor instead of chopping it.

Fry the beef with the lemongrass mixture for a minute before adding the fish sauce. This will help brown the meat and caramelise the lemongrass for good *wok hei*.

Taste any wok-fried dish before you finish cooking so you can adjust seasoning to suit your tastes.

BEEF WITH BROCCOLI AND OYSTER SAUCE

SERVES 4 PREPARATION TIME 10 MINS + 10 MINS MARINATING **COOKING TIME 15 MINS**

One of the most useful skills in wok cooking is blanching. Par-cooking vegetables before frying means they will cook faster and more completely when combined in the wok.

INGREDIENTS

500g rump steak, thinly sliced

2 tbsp peanut oil

2 cups broccoli florets

3 thin slices ginger, bruised

3 cloves garlic, peeled and roughly chopped

1 small onion, peeled and thinly sliced

¼ cup oyster sauce

1 tbsp soy sauce

2 tbsp stock or water

½ tsp sugar

1 tsp cornflour mixed with 1 tbsp cold stock or water

Chillies in Soy Sauce (page 29), to serve

Meat marinade

1 tbsp soy sauce

1 tbsp Shaoxing wine

1 tsp sesame oil

½ tsp cornflour

A pinch white pepper

METHOD

1   Combine the beef with the marinade ingredients and set aside for at least 10 minutes.

2   Heat a cup or two of water in the wok until boiling, add about a teaspoon of the oil and blanch the broccoli for about 1 minute, or until it is bright green and slightly softened. Remove and set aside until ready to fry.

3   Drain the water from the wok and dry the wok over the flame. Add the remaining oil and add the ginger first then the garlic to the oil, then the onion and fry until the onion is softened. Scoop the onion, garlic and ginger out of the oil and add to the broccoli.

4   Using the flavoured oil left in the wok, fry the beef in batches until well browned. Return all the ingredients back to the wok and toss together. Add the oyster sauce, soy sauce, stock and sugar and toss to coat. Slowly drizzle the cornflour mixture into the wok while tossing, until the liquids thicken and cling to the ingredients. Remove to a plate, rest for a minute and serve with rice and some Chillies in Soy Sauce.

NOTES

You don't need to cook the broccoli all the way through while blanching. Remember, you aren't stopping the cooking process with cold water so the broccoli will continue to cook after you take it out of the wok.

Oil-blanching is a popular technique in wok cooking in restaurants where meat or vegetables are boiled in oil before wok-frying. It tastes great, but I prefer to use water as the dish turns out less oily.

BEEF CHOW FUN

SERVES 2 PREPARATION TIME 15 MINS + 10 MINS MARINATING **COOKING TIME 10 MINS**

This classic Cantonese fried noodle dish is about as basic as it gets, but once you've become comfortable with it you can apply the same principles to making almost any fried noodles in your wok.

INGREDIENTS

160g beef rump or topside, very thinly sliced

2 tbsp peanut oil

3 thin slices ginger, bruised

2 cloves garlic, peeled and minced

¼ tsp salt

4 thick spring onions, trimmed, cut into 7cm lengths and sliced vertically

500g fresh wide flat rice noodles

1 tbsp dark soy sauce

1 tbsp soy sauce

A good pinch sugar

A good pinch white pepper

1 tbsp Shaoxing wine

2 cups beansprouts

Chillies in Soy Sauce (page 29), to serve

Marinade

2 tsp dark soy sauce

2 tsp Shaoxing wine

1 tsp sesame oil

1 tsp cornflour

METHOD

1 Mix the meat with the marinade ingredients and set aside for at least 10 minutes.

2 Heat a wok over high heat and add half the oil. Fry the meat until well browned and remove from the wok. Brush out the wok if necessary.

3 Add the remainder of the oil, the ginger, garlic, salt and spring onions, tossing until fragrant. Add the rice noodles, toss and allow to sit for a minute over heat without tossing, then add the soy sauces, sugar and pepper and pour in the Shaoxing wine around the edges of the wok. Toss for a further minute then add the beef. If the wok looks a little dry you can add some water, stock or oil to moisten. Toss occasionally until the noodles soften, then add the beansprouts and toss until they soften too. Serve with some Chillies in Soy Sauce.

NOTES

A two-person serve of this dish is about the most that should be cooked in a domestic wok in one batch to still achieve good *wok hei*.

Beansprouts are often included in dishes with noodles. The long, thin shape of beansprouts matches the noodle, but provides a crunch to give the dish a better texture.

When frying meat and vegetables with rice or noodles, the carbohydrate is the main element of the dish. Don't add too many other ingredients. A good rule of thumb is that the meat should weigh no more than one-third of the weight of the noodles.

SALT AND PEPPER PRAWNS

SERVES 4-6 FOR SHARING PREPARATION TIME 10 MINS **COOKING TIME 15 MINS**

The best thing about a wok is just how versatile it is. Rather than spending hundreds or even thousands of dollars on expensive pans or appliances, your wok can do just about anything you need in the kitchen. In this dish prawns are quickly shallow-fried, then stir-fried in one wok. It's one of my family's favourite dishes.

INGREDIENTS

8 large raw king prawns

2 tbsp cornflour

1 cup vegetable oil

2 small spring onions, trimmed and sliced

2 cloves garlic, peeled and roughly chopped

2 bird's-eye chillies, sliced

¼ tsp salt

¼ tsp ground white pepper

2 cups shredded iceberg lettuce, to serve

Lemon wedges, to serve

METHOD

1   Prepare the prawns by snipping off the front part of the heads behind the eyes with kitchen scissors, as well as the sharp spike at the centre of the fan of the tail. Cut through the back of each prawn and remove the intestine. Toss the prawns in the cornflour.

2   Add the oil to a hot wok and heat until the oil shimmers across its surface. Fry the prawns in batches for about 3 minutes each, or until cooked through and crisp. Drain the prawns on a wire rack and pour away most of the oil, leaving about a tablespoon in the base of the wok.

3   Add the spring onions, garlic and chillies and toss in the wok for 2 minutes, or until lightly browned and fragrant. Return the prawns to the wok and toss, seasoning with the salt and pepper until well mixed. Serve the prawns on the lettuce with lemon wedges.

NOTES

Prawns cooked in the shell have much more flavour than prawns peeled before cooking. You can eat as much or as little of the shell as you like. I tend to eat the crispy legs, shell and tail. The rest of my family likes nothing better than cracking the heads and sucking out the flavourful tomalley.

Don't coat the prawns with too much flour - it should only be the lightest of coatings. Skim the oil as much as you can to get rid of any bits of flour that shake off the prawns. If left in the oil from batch to batch, they will leave the dish with a burnt flavour and unsightly black specks.

These salt and pepper prawns may look different to the other wok-fried dishes in this lesson, but the principle is the same. Flavour the oil and use that to flavour the dish. In this case the oil is flavoured both by the prawns first and then the spring onions, garlic and chilli later.

SINGAPORE CHILLI CRAB

SERVES 2–4   PREPARATION TIME 20 MINS   **COOKING TIME 20 MINS**

In Chinese culture expensive dishes like mud crab, lobster, coral trout, abalone and suckling pig are commonly eaten at special occasions like birthdays, weddings, Chinese New Year, or when celebrating milestones or accomplishments. It's the Chinese equivalent of cracking open a bottle of French champagne.

INGREDIENTS

¼ cup vegetable oil

1 large mud crab, cleaned and cut into pieces (see pages 142–143)

¼ tsp salt

1 cup tomato passata

1 cup stock or water

2 tbsp palm sugar

1 tbsp white vinegar

1 tbsp soy sauce

3 thick spring onions, trimmed and cut into 5cm lengths

1 tsp cornflour mixed with 2 tbsp cold water

1 egg, beaten

½ cup loosely packed coriander, to serve

1 bird's-eye chilli, sliced, to serve

Rempah

6 eschalots or 1 medium onion, peeled and sliced

4 cloves garlic

6 large red chillies

1 tsp *belacan* (shrimp paste) (optional)

METHOD

1   Blend the ingredients for the *rempah* to a smooth paste. Heat a wok over medium heat and add the oil. Fry the *rempah* for about 5 minutes, or until fragrant and the oil separates from the solids.

2   Add the crab pieces and salt and toss until the crab starts to change colour. Add the passata, stock, sugar, vinegar and soy sauce and toss to coat. Stir in the crab tomalley (see below). Cover the wok and simmer for 10 minutes. Add the spring onions and toss through. Taste the crab and adjust seasoning. Drizzle the cornflour mixture slowly into the wok while stirring, then drizzle the egg mixture slowly into the wok while stirring. The egg should form wispy threads and thicken the chilli mixture. Remove the crab and sauce to a plate, scatter with coriander and sliced chilli and serve.

NOTES

Cracking the crab claws allows the flavour of the sauce to penetrate the crab, but it also helps the flavour from the shell to combine with the sauce. The pleasure of eating a whole crab dish is in the thrill of the chase. Every delicious morsel must be hunted for and painstakingly extracted. Take your time with it.

The function of a liver and pancreas in a crab is carried out by a yellowish paste known as the 'tomalley'. It's prized in every Asian culture. Stirring it into the sauce of this dish provides a rich flavour.

LESSON 5
RICE AND NOODLES

Rice and noodles are the main staples of nearly every Asian cuisine, and there are many different varieties.

These starches are more than just fillers for the belly. They are a light textural component of a meal, offsetting the strong textures of meat or vegetable dishes. They are also palate cleansers, allowing you to move from one dish to another in a shared meal without confusing flavours. And they are even flavours themselves; the best rices have fragrant grainy, sweet and even popcorn-like aromas, and noodles can have a range of flavours depending on their ingredients – from nutty buckwheat or rich egg noodles, to milky or starchy rice or wheat noodles. Rice and noodles are far more than just bland accompaniments. Knowing what to do with them is vital to good Asian cookery.

It's hard to overstate just how important well-cooked rice or noodles are to Asian food. Imagine Italian cuisine without its pasta, or French without its magnificent breads. That might give you an idea of what a bowl of good rice might mean to a Chinese meal, or what role the elegant simplicity of a serving of Cold Udon Noodles (page 111) plays in the cuisine of Japan.

1

2

3

4

5

6a

6b

Thick rice noodles – These popular noodles form the base of many regional specialities, from Cantonese Beef Chow Fun (page 89), Thailand's *pad see ew*, *hu tieu* in Vietnam, or my favourite, the classic *char kway teow* from Penang, where I was born in Malaysia. They are available both fresh or dried and, when cooked well, the texture should be soft and chewy but never mushy. **1**

Thin rice noodles (dried) – Made from the same ingredients as the thick rice noodles, thin, flat rice noodles, also known as 'rice stick noodles', are used in dishes like Pad Thai (page 45) or Fish Ball Noodle Soup (page 147). **2**

Rice vermicelli – Thin vermicelli-style rice noodles are found all over Southeast Asia and are very popular in Vietnamese cuisine. Try them in dishes like Bun Cha (page 115). **3**

Mung bean vermicelli – Also called 'glass noodles' or 'cellophane noodles' for their clear and shiny appearance when cooked, vermicelli made from mung bean flour have a chewier texture than rice vermicelli. When dry they look very similar, but don't confuse them, they're used quite differently. **4**

Thick egg noodle (Hokkien) – Hokkien noodles or 'oil noodles' are made from wheat flour and egg or water that has been alkalised with lye. They often have a yellow appearance from the egg used. The alkalised water inhibits gluten, allowing the noodles to be stretched and giving them a slippery texture. Their thickness and weight makes them perfect for heavier-flavoured fried noodle dishes. **5**

Thin egg noodles – Thin egg or alkaline noodles are also popular made as fried noodle dishes, as well as in noodle soups. This versatile noodle is used for Japan's iconic ramen noodles, but is also hugely popular for many purposes all around Asia. They are available both fresh **6a** and dried. **6b**

Wheat noodles - Wheat noodles made without egg have a lighter appearance and are usually made from just wheat flour and water. **7**

Soba - Japanese soba noodles are made from buckwheat flour and are available in Australia in their dried form. They're often served cold, just boiled and drained with a dipping sauce, or sometimes in a light broth. They are rarely fried. **8**

Udon - Thick Japanese udon wheat noodles are eaten cold with a dipping sauce (see page 111), but their thick, chewy texture means they stand up to use in strongly flavoured dishes. They are available fresh **9a**, frozen and dried. **9b**

Rice paper - Dried rice papers are used to wrap fresh ingredients for Rice Paper Rolls (page 120), or the Vietnamese version of Spring Rolls (page 119). **10**

Spring roll wrappers - Spring roll wrappers made from wheat flour are used to wrap Chinese spring rolls. They're readily available frozen from Asian grocers and some supermarkets. **11**

Wonton skins - Wontons are simple dumplings commonly used for soup. The skins are usually made from an egg pastry similar to Italian pasta. **12**

Gow gee wrappers - *Gow gee*, *jiaozi*, and *gyoza* are all variations of the same Chinese word meaning 'dumpling' (in Cantonese, Mandarin and Japanese respectively). These basic flour and water wrappers are available in pre-rolled packs, but it's very easy to make your own. They form the wrapping for the simple, home-style Boiled Dumplings on page 106. **13**

RICE

SERVES 4-6 PREPARATION TIME 5 MINS **COOKING TIME 20 MINS**

Cooking rice is fundamental to good Asian food, and luckily it's quite simple.
Just choose the variety of rice that best suits your meal, and follow these simple steps.

INGREDIENTS

3-4 cups short-grain, jasmine or
    glutinous rice

METHOD

1 Wash the rice well by placing it in a bowl or pot and covering it with water. Agitate the grains with your hands to remove excess starch and pour away the milky water, taking care not to pour away any of the rice. Repeat three or four times until the discarded water is nearly clear.

2 *For short-grain or jasmine rice*: In a medium saucepan, cover the rice with cold water to about 2cm above the top of the rice. Many people measure this by placing the tip of their finger at the top of the rice and adding water until it reaches the line of their first knuckle. You can leave the rice to soak at this stage if you wish, or just cook it immediately. Bring the rice and water to a vigorous boil and boil until the water absorbs to reach the top of the rice. Small holes should appear in the surface where steam escapes. Cover the pot and reduce the heat to as low as possible and cook for 12 minutes. Turn off the heat and allow the pot to stand, still covered, for a further 5 minutes. Remove the lid and cut through the rice with a rice paddle or serving spoon to turn it in the pot, separate the grains and allow excess steam to escape. Allow to stand uncovered for 1 minute, then cover the pot again and keep warm until ready to serve.

   For glutinous rice: Line a bamboo steamer with muslin. Place the washed rice in a mound in the centre and place the steamer over a pot of boiling water. Steam the rice for 10 minutes, then roll the rice over in the muslin so that the top is now at the bottom. Steam for a further 10 minutes.

NOTES

By far the easiest way to cook rice is to use a rice cooker. Most Asian families will have one and they're great for both cooking rice and keeping it warm from one meal to the next.

Never cook less than 2 cups of rice at a time. It won't turn out right.

When cooking rice on the stove it's best to use a heavy saucepan. Even, gentle heat is perfect for giving the rice time to absorb liquid.

CUCUMBER AND TUNA SUSHI ROLLS
Kappamaki to tekkamaki

SERVES 2-4 PREPARATION TIME 30 MINS **COOKING TIME 20 MINS**

While thick rolls (*futomaki*) with multiple ingredients have become the norm in sushi restaurants in the West, sushi rolls in Japanese sushi restaurants are more commonly thin rolls (*hosomaki*) containing just a single ingredient. These cucumber and tuna versions are the most common varieties, and are found all over Japan.

INGREDIENTS

4 sheets nori

2 Lebanese cucumbers

150g sashimi-grade tuna

2 tsp wasabi, plus extra, to serve

Soy sauce, to serve

Pickled ginger, to serve

Sushi rice

3 cups short-grain *koshihikari* rice

1 piece kombu (optional)

½ cup rice vinegar

2 tbsp caster sugar

1 tsp salt

METHOD

1   For the sushi rice, wash and cook the rice as set out on page 100. If using kombu, place it in the cold water just as the rice begins to cook and remove it when the water begins to steam – before it comes to the boil. Place the rice vinegar, caster sugar and salt in a small saucepan and place over low heat, stirring until the solids dissolve.

2   When the rice is cooked and rested, tip it into a large, deep tray and fluff the rice with a cutting motion of a rice paddle. Rapidly cool it with a fan and drive off excess steam. Sprinkle over a little of the vinegar mixture and continue to fluff and fan the rice to mix it through. Continue adding the vinegar and fluffing the rice until it reaches blood temperature, i.e. when it feels slightly warm when you touch it with your knuckles. Cover the rice with a damp tea towel until ready to use.

3   *Kappamaki*: Peel the cucumber in strips and remove the seeds. Cut the cucumber lengthways into long strips with a 1cm square cross-section.

   Tekkamaki: Cut long lengths of tuna with a 1cm square cross-section.

4   Prepare a small bowl of cool water seasoned with a little vinegar and use it to dampen your hands. To roll the sushi, divide a piece of nori in half and place one half shiny side-down on a sushi mat. Take about ¾ of a cup of sushi rice and spread it in a thin, even layer over the nori, leaving a 1cm border at the top of the mat. The preferred way of doing this is to place the rice in the top left corner of the nori (leaving a 1cm gap from the top) and 'pull' the mass of rice across the nori to the right to create a thick band

of rice through the centre of the nori. Then 'roll' the band down to the base of the nori. The rice should be around ¾cm thick across the nori, with the nori still visible in places through the rice.

5 Lay a single line of cucumber (*kappamaki*) or tuna (*tekkamaki*) along the same line. For tekkamaki it is common to add wasabi. Just smear a little wasabi paste through the centre of the rice and place the tuna on top.

6 Roll the rice up around the filling so that the bottom of the rectangle of rice reaches the top. Press firmly and evenly along the length of the mat. Continue rolling to complete the roll, then place the roll on a cutting board and use the mat to ensure the roll is firm and uniform. If any rice is sticking out the end of the roll, push it back in with your fingers.

7 With a dampened knife, cut the rolls into half, then cut each half in thirds to create six small thin rolls. Serve with soy sauce (or Tosa Joyu, page 57), a little extra wasabi, and pickled ginger.

NOTES

Making the vinegared rice for sushi is the most important step in this process. The grains should be separate but slightly sticking together with a glossy appearance.

The pickled ginger acts as a palate cleanser between mouthfuls. It is often dyed pink to mimic the natural pink tinge that tender young ginger has when pickled. If your ginger is yellow or just very slightly blushed with pink, you can be confident it hasn't been dyed.

If you prefer to make thick rolls just use a whole sheet of nori and fill the sheet with rice. Use three or four different ingredients for each thick roll.

In Japan, sushi rice is fanned and mixed in a specific wooden basin to keep the rice moist and fluffy. If you don't have one, just use a deep bowl or baking tray.

BOILED DUMPLINGS
Shui jiao

MAKES ABOUT 75 DUMPLINGS PREPARATION TIME 1-2 HOURS **COOKING TIME 5 MINS**

It's easy to be intimidated by the thought of dumplings when you see the artistic and delicately folded masterpieces at *yum cha (dim sum)*. But dumplings are not just the domain of the chef – they were a mainstay of the home kitchen long before chefs got their hands on them. You'd be hard-pressed to find a Chinese family without a pack of homemade dumplings in the freezer. If you want to get in on the act, these simple boiled dumplings are the perfect place for you to start.

INGREDIENTS

1 portion Hot Water Dough (see below),
   or 75 *gow gee* wrappers
Chinkiang black vinegar, chilli oil,
   soy sauce, and sliced spring onions,
   to serve

Basic filling

1kg pork mince
100g Chinese cabbage, finely chopped
5 thin spring onions, finely chopped
4 garlic cloves, peeled and finely
   chopped
1½ tsp salt
2 tbsp soy sauce
1 tbsp Shaoxing wine
1 tsp sesame oil

Hot water dough

4 cups plain flour
2 cups boiling water

METHOD

1   For the hot water dough, place the flour in the bowl of a stand mixer with the dough hook attachment. Gradually add the boiling water until the flour comes together into a dough. Run the mixer to knead for 5 minutes until the dough is smooth. Place in a plastic bag and squeeze out as much air as you can. Rest for at least 30 minutes before using.

2   For the dumpling filling, place all the ingredients in a pot or large bowl and stir in a single direction until well combined. Refrigerate until ready to use.

3   When you're ready to make the dumplings, start by rolling a few skins at a time. Pinch off a handful of dough and roll it into a sausage shape of 2cm diameter. Cut the sausage into 2cm lengths. Stand each length on its cut end and squash down to create a disc. To roll the dumpling skins, use a very thin rolling pin or a short length of dowel on a floured surface and roll with one hand, applying pressure only when rolling into the centre of the dough, turning the disc with your other hand each roll to create a uniform circle about 10cm in diameter and 1mm thin. The centre should be slightly thicker than the edges.

4   Flatten about a teaspoon of filling in the centre of the skin and fold the dumpling as you like. For the simple fold shown on the next page, first pinch together the top and bottom of the wrapper. Then with the 'v' between your thumb and index finger of your left hand, pinch the dumpling, creating a fold on the index-finger side. Without letting go of the dumpling with your left hand, pinch the other side of the dumpling with your right hand, also creating a fold on the index-finger side. The dumpling should be straight along your thumbs, pleated along your index fingers, and sit upright when placed on a flat surface.

5 Lay the folded dumplings on a lined tray and put them in the freezer when the tray is full. When the dough is firm enough to handle without sticking, you can transfer the dumplings to a freezer bag. They will keep for six months frozen.

6 To cook the dumplings (fresh or frozen), boil them for about 5 minutes until they rise to the top of the water. Scoop the dumplings from the water with a slotted spoon or sieve, and serve with black vinegar, chilli oil, spring onions and a little soy sauce if you like.

NOTES

Try replacing half the pork with chopped prawn meat, or add flavourings such as herbs, chilli, pea shoots, spinach, water chestnuts, or even cold jellied stock to make dumplings that will be full of soup when cooked.

I make the dumpling filling in a heavy saucepan because the steep sides keep the filling in the bowl when mixing.

As mentioned in the method, stir the dumpling mixture in one direction only. This will align the proteins in the meat for a stronger textured filling.

Use a butter knife or small spatula to transfer the filling to the skin. It's much easier than using a teaspoon.

Folding pleats helps the shape but you may also need to slightly mould the dumplings with your hands after folding to make sure the skins are thin and the shape is correct. My grandmother tastes the filling raw to check for seasoning. If that's not for you, I suggest boiling or even microwaving just a pinch to check the seasoning before you fold all the dumplings.

If you're new to making dumplings, try using store-bought skins first as they are easier to handle, making it easier to practise folding. Bought skins need water for sealing and are more firm. Handmade skins are softer and can be pinched together for a good seal without needing extra water. In my view, the handmade skins produce a much tastier dumpling.

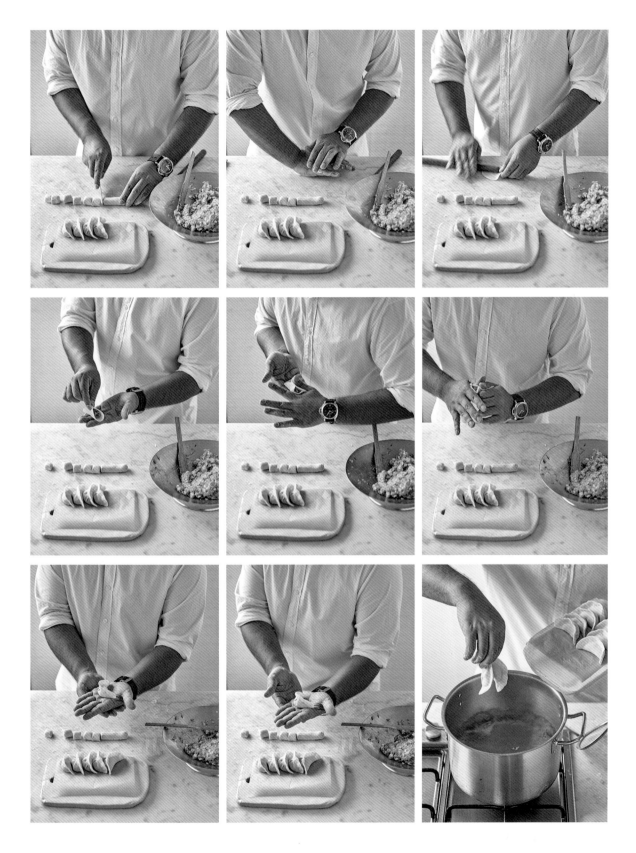

COLD UDON NOODLES
Zaru udon

SERVES 2 PREPARATION TIME 15 MINS **COOKING TIME 15 MINS**

This dish from Japanese cuisine illustrates how noodles are the centre of a dish rather than an accompaniment. Just noodles, a dip and a few condiments make for a meal that's perfect in its simplicity.

INGREDIENTS

500g udon noodles

½ sheet nori, cut into thirds then finely sliced

2 tbsp finely sliced thin spring onions

1 tsp grated ginger, to serve

2 tsp sesame seeds, to serve

Mentsuyu noodle dip

2 cups Bonito Stock (page 32)

¼ cup mirin

¼ cup soy sauce

METHOD

1   For the *mentsuyu* noodle dip, combine the ingredients in a saucepan and bring to a simmer. Simmer for 1 minute then remove from the heat and set aside.

2   To make the noodles, bring a large pot of water to the boil and prepare two large bowls, one with cold water and one with iced water. Cook the udon noodles according to the packet directions, then strain in a deep strainer and plunge into cold water, shaking the strainer vigorously to quickly cool the noodles. Next plunge the strainer into the iced water to chill the noodles.

3   Place the noodles on four flat bamboo strainers to serve and top with the nori. If you don't have flat strainers for serving, plates will be fine, but make sure the noodles are well-drained. Divide the noodle dip between four small bowls. Serve the spring onions, ginger and sesame seeds on individual small plates on the side. To eat, mix the condiments with the noodle dip, dip a few noodles into it and enjoy.

NOTES

You could make these with soba noodles instead of udon. Cook the noodles according to the packet directions, replace the grated ginger with wasabi and leave out the nori.

This dish is best eaten with chopsticks. Japanese people eat noodles with a slurp, sucking up noodles and sauce or soup together, whether hot or cold. They say the slurping action slightly aerates the soup or sauce, giving the dish a better texture.

Although a portion of noodles is a meal in itself, this is also great paired with a small portion of Mixed Tempura (page 54).

SALMON RICE BALLS
Sake no onigiri

MAKES 6 RICE BALLS PREPARATION TIME 10 MINS

Outside Japan sushi is synonymous with Japanese cuisine, but within its borders without question the most popular food are *onigiri* – rice balls. Parents pack them for kids' school lunches and adults take them on road trips. Anywhere, any time of day, *onigiri* are the soul of Japanese food.

INGREDIENTS

100g leftover Salt-grilled Salmon (page 155)

3 cups cooked short-grain rice, warm

1 tsp salt

2 sheets nori, cut into rectangular strips 5cm × 10cm

METHOD

1   Break the salmon into small chunks and mix with the rice.

2   Wet your hands and sprinkle a little salt onto both palms. Take one-sixth of the rice and salmon mix and gently mould it into a thick puck shape with cupped hands. Don't mash the rice together, just press it together enough so that it holds its shape.

3   Wrap the rice ball with a rectangle of nori. The *onigiri* can be served immediately or wrapped in foil for transport. They shouldn't be refrigerated, as that will make the rice dry and hard.

NOTES

Rather than making rice balls with salmon, you can fill them with other ingredients instead. Just mould the rice ball halfway, press a hollow into the centre and fill with your choice of ingredients. Then complete moulding the rice ball to completely encase them.

Popular fillings for rice balls include tinned cooked tuna mixed with mayonnaise, and pickled plum (*ume*).

The rice balls can also be grilled. Just place on a hot grill or lightly oiled frypan and baste with a little soy sauce until crisp and browned on the outside.

BUN CHA
Vietnamese pork patties with rice noodles

SERVES 4 PREPARATION TIME 20 MINS + 30 MINS REFRIGERATION **COOKING TIME 15 MINS**

A street food favourite in Vietnam, *bun cha* is a dish characterised by contrasts. Meaty, caramelised patties contrast with fresh herbs and vegetables, and soft noodles contrast with crunchy fried spring rolls. It's all tied together by that most versatile of Vietnamese sauces, *nuoc cham*.

INGREDIENTS

500g pork mince

2 tbsp fish sauce

1 tbsp caster sugar

1 tbsp honey

6 thin spring onions, trimmed and finely chopped (white and light green parts)

3 cloves garlic, peeled and minced

½ tsp salt

¼ tsp ground black pepper

200g dried rice vermicelli noodles

4 cups beansprouts

Green oak lettuce, mint, coriander and Thai basil, to serve

8 small Vietnamese Spring Rolls (page 119), to serve (optional)

Sauce

1 cup Nuoc Cham, undiluted (page 28)

1 cup water

½ small carrot, peeled and thinly sliced into rounds

10cm daikon, peeled and cut into thin strips

METHOD

1   Mix together the pork, fish sauce, sugar, honey, spring onions, garlic, salt and pepper and stir until well combined. Set aside in the fridge for at least 30 minutes.

2   For the sauce, mix together all of the ingredients and allow to stand for 5 minutes.

3   Heat a well-oiled frypan or barbecue grill on low-medium heat. With wet hands, form the pork mixture into small balls the size of ping pong balls and squash them into thick, flat patties. Fry or grill the patties for about 3-5 minutes on each side, or until well caramelised and cooked through. Keep warm until ready to serve.

4   Soak the rice noodles in plenty of cold water for 15 minutes, or until they are softened. Bring additional water to the boil in a large saucepan and boil the noodles for a minute until cooked. Drain very well and divide into individual bowls. Blanch the beansprouts for a minute, drain and add to the bowls. Place a few patties in each bowl with plenty of lettuce leaves, fresh herbs and a few small spring rolls, if using. Serve with a bowl of the sauce on the side.

NOTES

If your heat is too high when cooking the patties, the sugars will blacken and caramelise long before they are cooked inside.

You could use other varieties of herbs as well if you prefer. Vietnamese mint and perilla (*shiso*) would be good choices.

COLD SESAME NOODLES
Ma jiang mian

SERVES 4 PREPARATION TIME 20 MINS **COOKING TIME 20 MINS**

These Taiwanese noodles are all about the dressing – rich and flavourful, but slightly tart. Just the dressing and noodles together is a popular meal itself, but adding a few toppings is my favourite way to eat them.

INGREDIENTS

500g fresh thin wheat or egg noodles

1 carrot, cut into fine matchsticks

2 Lebanese cucumbers, peeled in strips and cut into fine matchsticks

2 cups shredded cooked chicken or ham

Peanut and sesame dressing

4 tbsp sesame seeds, toasted

¼ cup unsalted roasted peanuts

1½ tbsp caster sugar

¼ cup soy sauce

¼ cup sesame oil

¼ cup Chinkiang black vinegar

¼ cup cold water

Shredded omelette

3 eggs, beaten

A pinch salt

1 tsp sesame oil

2 tsp peanut oil

METHOD

1 For the shredded omelette, mix the eggs with the salt and sesame oil. Heat a wok or frypan and grease with the peanut oil. Add the egg and rotate the wok or pan to create a very thin layer of egg. When the egg sets, remove from the wok and allow to cool. Roll the egg into a cylinder and slice thinly.

2 For the dressing, pound the sesame seeds and peanuts with a mortar and pestle to a smooth paste. Add the remaining dressing ingredients and mix well.

3 Cook the noodles according to the packet directions and rinse under cold running water. Drain well. Place on a plate with piles of carrot, cucumber, chicken or ham and shredded egg. Pour over the dressing, mix and serve.

NOTES

Different types and brands of noodles will vary in the amount they swell during cooking. Some that have been par-cooked will only increase in size slightly whereas others that are cooked from raw may expand a lot.

To make 2 cups of shredded chicken breast, place 2 chicken breasts in a pot of cold water, cover and bring to the boil. Turn off the heat and leave for 5-7 minutes. Drain, then shred the meat with your fingers.

The key to this dish is the texture. Take as much care as you can to shred the vegetables and chicken finely. It will make a world of difference.

VIETNAMESE SPRING ROLLS
Nem ran

MAKES 40 SPRING ROLLS PREPARATION TIME 1 HOUR + 20 MINS SOAKING **COOKING TIME 30 MINS**

Originally a celebratory food in China symbolising wealth through their resemblance to gold bars, 'spring rolls' are now everywhere in Asia. From the original Chinese *chun juan* have come the *popiah* of Taiwan, Malaysia and Indonesia, *lumpiah* in the Philippines, and even these Vietnamese *nem ran*.

INGREDIENTS

40 spring roll wrappers, or rice papers softened in cold water

2 eggs, beaten

About 2 litres vegetable oil, for deep-frying

Nuoc Cham (page 28) and lettuce leaves, to serve

Filling

150g mung bean vermicelli

50g dried wood ear mushrooms

500g pork mince

500g raw prawns, peeled and roughly chopped

2 small carrots, finely shredded

1 medium brown onion, peeled and minced

3 cloves garlic, peeled and minced

1 tsp salt

2 tbsp fish sauce

2 tsp sugar

½ tsp white pepper

METHOD

1 In separate bowls, pour boiling water over the noodles and mushrooms and allow to soak for 10 minutes for the noodles and 20 minutes for the mushrooms. Drain both, cut the mushrooms into thin strips and cut the noodles into 2cm lengths. Combine in a large bowl with the remaining filling ingredients and stir well.

2 Take a spring roll wrapper and lay about 2 tbsp of filling diagonally in a line near one corner. Roll towards the opposite corner, moulding the roll into a cylinder as you go, folding in the sides just before the centre of the wrapper. Seal the end of the roll with a small amount of beaten egg. Repeat for the remaining rolls.

3 Heat the oil in a saucepan or wok to 170°C. Fry the spring rolls for 6 minutes (fresh) or 8 minutes (frozen), turning occasionally until the spring rolls are golden brown and cooked through. Transfer to a wire rack to drain. Serve the spring rolls with Nuoc Cham and lettuce leaves.

NOTES

If this is your first time making Vietnamese spring rolls, use the Chinese wheat-based wrappers instead of rice paper. They are much easier to use when folding the rolls, and less temperamental when frying.

Shredded taro root or *jicama* (yam bean) is often used as part of the filling. If you can find some, give it a try.

Spring rolls are excellent to freeze raw. You can fry them straight from the freezer without needing to defrost them first.

RICE PAPER ROLLS
Goi cuon

SERVES 4-6 PREPARATION TIME 20 MINS **COOKING TIME 20 MINS**

Although I love Vietnamese fried spring rolls, these fresh rice paper rolls are my favourite rolls to eat. They're light and delicious and hugely popular in Vietnam as well as all around the world.

INGREDIENTS

300g pork belly, skin and bone removed

1 tbsp salt

100g dried rice vermicelli

30 rice paper sheets

3 cups shredded iceberg lettuce

1 cup loosely packed mint

1 cup loosely packed coriander or perilla

300g cooked prawns, peeled, deveined
    and split lengthways

1 bunch Chinese chives, halved

1 cup Nuoc Cham (page 28), to serve

METHOD

1   Place the pork belly in a pot just big enough to fit it. Cover with cold water. Add the salt, bring the water to a simmer and simmer for 20 minutes, or until the pork belly is cooked through. Remove from the water and allow to cool. Thinly slice the pork into 5cm wide slices no more than a few millimetres thick.

2   Place the rice vermicelli in a large bowl and pour over plenty of boiling water. Leave for 5 minutes then drain, rinse in cold water, drain again and cut into 5cm lengths.

3   Fill a large bowl with lukewarm water and dip a sheet of rice paper into the water until it slightly softens. (It will continue to soften out of the water.) Transfer the rice paper to a plate and place a pile of pork, lettuce, rice vermicelli and some mint and coriander on the paper in a line just in from the edge closest to you. Place a few prawns at the centre of the paper with the orange backs facing down and roll the paper, folding in the edges halfway along, as shown. Add a few spears of chives just before finishing the roll so the cut ends stick out of the top. Serve with Nuoc Cham.

NOTES

Keeping the prawns separate from the other fillings is purely for presentation, so you can see the colourful backs facing outward through a single layer of rice paper.

You don't need to do all the work yourself - you can put the ingredients on platters on the dining table with bowls of warm water to dip the rice papers into and everyone can make their own.

The filling of the rolls can be whatever you like. Try leftover Lemongrass Beef (page 85), shredded chicken, or even the pork patties from Bun Cha (page 115).

INDONESIAN CHICKEN FRIED RICE
Nasi goreng ayam

SERVES 4   PREPARATION TIME 15 MINS   **COOKING TIME 10 MINS**

Indonesian *nasi goreng* demonstrates the strong sweet and savoury flavours that are common in Indonesian food. If you've ever been to Indonesia, this is probably already one of your favourite dishes.

INGREDIENTS

¼ cup vegetable oil

250g chicken thigh fillets, thinly sliced

100g green beans, trimmed and sliced into ½cm lengths

1 tbsp palm sugar, chopped

8 cups cooked jasmine rice (preferably refrigerated overnight)

½ tsp salt

¼ cup *kecap manis*

2 tbsp soy sauce

2 tbsp tomato sauce

2 eggs

1 Lebanese cucumber, sliced, to serve

Prawn crackers, to serve (optional)

Paste

3 eschalots or 1 small brown onion, peeled and sliced

3 cloves garlic

1 bird's-eye chilli, or to taste

2 tsp *belacan* (shrimp paste)

METHOD

1   Combine the paste ingredients and pound to a smooth paste with a mortar and pestle or food processor.

2   Heat a wok over high heat until smoking and add the vegetable oil. Fry the paste for about 3 minutes, until very fragrant. Add the chicken and toss to coat in the paste. Add the beans and palm sugar and toss well. Add the rice, salt, *kecap manis*, soy sauce and tomato sauce and mix well, pressing the rice against the sides of the wok to separate the grains. Move the rice to one side of the wok and crack the eggs into the open side. Mix to break up the yolks and allow to half-set. Combine the eggs and rice and remove from the heat. Serve with sliced cucumbers and prawn crackers, if using.

NOTES

In Asian cuisines fried rice is almost always a meal or course in itself. It is rarely eaten as an accompaniment to other dishes because it can overpower other flavours.

You can cook prawn crackers very easily without deep-frying them. Just place them in the microwave for about 20 seconds on high and watch them puff before your eyes.

Even in a dish as simple as fried rice, texture and contrast are important. The crunch of the prawn crackers and the freshness of cucumber are not just afterthoughts, they are the key to making this a complete dish.

LESSON 6
VEGETABLES

Vegetables are often at the centre of an Asian meal, forming much of its volume where meat and fish are used as flavourings rather than the focus.

The flavour of vegetables themselves is used to season dishes. Sweet vegetables provide a foil to the sour soup in dishes like Pork Sinigang (page 41) in Filipino cuisine. Chinese cabbage is often used as a source of umami in wok-fried dishes, stews and soups like the Pork Belly, Cabbage and Shiitake Hotpot on page 13. With such a wide variety of vegetables and herbs used in Asian cuisines, the palette of flavours and textures available to you when cooking with vegetables is enormous.

Of course, these days people are better off than they used to be and meat production is more efficient. While that's made meat much more accessible across Asia, vegetables are still at the very heart of Asian food.

The names of Asian vegetables and herbs in English can sometimes be confusing. Many of them come from different dialects of Chinese and other Asian languages and there is little consistency in how those names are applied. Just follow the visual guide on the following pages to make sure you're getting what you're looking for.

Chinese cabbage - Also known as *wombok*, napa cabbage or *baicai*, this is one of my favourite vegetables. It is extremely nutrient dense and is also high in umami. **1**

Chinese broccoli - Also known as *gailan*, Chinese broccoli is a leafy, thick-stemmed green vegetable common in Chinese, Korean, Thai and Vietnamese cuisine. Its taste is similar to Western broccoli, and in fact broccolini is a hybrid between the two vegetables. **2**

Spinach - Spinach is a popular vegetable in almost all Asian cuisines. It is often wok-fried in Chinese dishes, or quickly blanched and dressed in Japanese and Korean cooking. **3**

Pak choy - *Pak choy* is a short, leafy cabbage-like green with light green stems and leaves. *Pak choy* and *bok choy* are different varieties of the same vegetable, and sometimes the names can be used interchangeably. **4**

Bok choy - *Bok choy* is longer than *pak choy* with a white stem and dark green leaves. Baby *bok choy* is also available, which looks very similar to *pak choy* but with slightly slimmer leaves. **5**

Water spinach - Known as *ong choy* in Cantonese and *kangkung* in Malaysia, this vegetable is popular all over Asia. The hollow stems and long leaves have a great texture and flavour. It's very popular fried with strong flavours in Southeast Asian cooking. **6**

Beansprouts - Beansprouts are the sprouts of the mung bean. They can be used just as they are, with no need to remove the small bean at one end or the hair-like 'tail' at the other. Soybean sprouts are also sometimes sold as beansprouts, and are identifiable by their larger, hard yellowish bean at one end. Store them in the fridge soaking in a large bowl of water. **7**

Pickled mustard greens - Mustard greens are a slightly bitter green vegetable similar to *bok choy*. They can be cooked and eaten fresh, but are also often pickled. I keep pickled mustard greens in my pantry to use if I don't have any fresh vegetables on hand. **8**

Chinese chives – Known as *jiucai* in China, *nira* in Japan and *buchu* in Korea, these long, flat, grass-like vegetables have a flavour that is similar to both garlic and onion. They have many uses, but are particularly good in wok-fried dishes, soups and dumplings. **9**

Spring onions – Spring onions are very popular in all Asian cuisines. I prefer to buy a mixture of thick and thin spring onions, as they can be used for different purposes. Thick spring onions are more suited to cooking, while thin-stemmed spring onions are more delicate when used raw. **10**

Vietnamese mint – This fragrant herb is known as *rau ram* in Vietnam and laksa leaf in Malaysia and Singapore. It's a key component to the popular spicy coconut milk laksa and Vietnamese salads. **11**

Thai basil – Thai basil has a sharper, stronger flavour than sweet basil, with slight notes of aniseed in its flavour. It's commonly used in Thai cuisine but also pops up elsewhere around Asia, even as a key flavouring in Taiwanese Popcorn Chicken (page 62). **12**

Coriander – Coriander is used all around Southeast Asia for its sharp, distinctive fragrance. The entire plant can be used, although the flavour of the leaves is very slightly different to that of the stems and roots. **13**

Perilla – Perilla (*shiso*) is used in many Vietnamese and Japanese dishes. Its flavour is sometimes described as a cross between cinnamon and mint. There are red and green varieties. **14**

Sesame leaf – Despite its name, this leaf from Korean cuisine isn't related to the sesame plant at all. It's a variety of perilla with a mild apple/aniseed flavour, and is used both raw and cooked or pickled. It's available from Korean grocers. **15**

BANCHAN

A full Korean meal wouldn't be complete without *banchan*, a selection of smaller plates or bowls on the table to share. It's probably technically accurate to call *banchan* 'side dishes', but their importance to Korean cuisine is so much more than that name implies. Although not all *banchan* are vegetable-based, here are some of my favourites.

BEANSPROUT SOUP
Kongnamulguk

SERVES 4
PREPARATION TIME 5 MINS
COOKING TIME 20 MINS

INGREDIENTS
1 tbsp sesame oil
3 cups beansprouts
1½ tsp salt
2 cloves garlic, peeled and minced
1 litre Anchovy Stock (page 33)
3 thin spring onions, trimmed and finely sliced, to serve

METHOD
1 Heat a medium pot over medium heat and add the sesame oil. Add the beansprouts and salt and fry for just a minute, or until the beansprouts begin to soften. Add the garlic and fry for a further minute until it is fragrant.

2 Add the Anchovy Stock and bring to a simmer. Cover and simmer for 15 minutes. Divide the soup among four bowls and scatter with spring onions to serve.

SPINACH NAMUL
Sigeumchi namul

MAKES ABOUT 2 CUPS
PREPARATION TIME 5 MINS
COOKING TIME 1 MIN

INGREDIENTS
1 bunch spinach (about 200g), washed and roots removed
2 cloves garlic, peeled and minced
1 thick spring onion, trimmed and finely minced
¼ tsp salt
1 tsp soy sauce
2 tsp sesame oil
1 tsp toasted sesame seeds

METHOD
1 Bring a pot of salted water to a rolling boil and add the spinach, root ends first. Blanch for just 30 seconds then remove and rinse in cold water. Strain, and squeeze out as much water as possible.

2 Combine the garlic, spring onion and salt and with the flat of your knife mash them together to a rough paste. Transfer the paste to a bowl and add the squeezed spinach. Pour over the soy sauce, sesame oil and sesame seeds and mix well.

POTATOES BRAISED IN SOY SAUCE
Gamja jorim

MAKES ABOUT 2 CUPS
PREPARATION TIME 15 MINS
COOKING TIME 20 MINS

INGREDIENTS

1 tbsp vegetable oil

2 large potatoes, peeled, cut into 2cm cubes and soaked in cold water for 10 minutes

½ tsp salt

1 small onion, peeled and cut into chunks

2 cloves garlic, peeled and minced

¼ cup soy sauce

1 tbsp sugar

1 tbsp Korean corn syrup, honey or an extra tbsp sugar

1 cup water

1 tsp toasted sesame seeds, to serve

METHOD

1 Heat a large frypan with a lid over medium heat and add the vegetable oil. Add the potatoes and salt and fry for about 3 minutes, or until warm and starting to cook. Add the onion and garlic and toss for a further 2 minutes, or until the onion begins to soften. Add the soy sauce, sugar and corn syrup and toss to coat.

2 Add the water, bring to a simmer and simmer, covered, for 10 minutes, tossing occasionally until the potatoes are softened. Remove the lid and reduce any remaining liquid for a minute or two. Scatter with sesame seeds and serve. (I prefer this dish served at room temperature.)

STUFFED CUCUMBER KIMCHI
Oi sobagi

MAKES ABOUT 4 CUPS
PREPARATION TIME 20 MINS
+ 1 HOUR STANDING

INGREDIENTS

8 Lebanese cucumbers, or Japanese or Korean cucumbers

3 tbsp salt

4 thick spring onions, white and light green part only, trimmed and finely shredded

1 small carrot, peeled and finely shredded

½ bunch Chinese chives (about 60g), trimmed and cut into 1cm lengths

5 cloves garlic, peeled and minced

1 tsp minced ginger

2 tbsp Korean chilli powder (*gochugaru*)

1 tbsp fish sauce

1 tsp toasted sesame seeds, to serve

METHOD

1 Peel a few strips of the skin from each of the Lebanese cucumbers. (If using Japanese or Korean cucumbers you don't need to peel them.) Trim the ends of the cucumbers and halve them. Cut a deep cross into the halved ends, leaving just 1cm of cucumber attached at the base.

2 Rub the salt into the cucumbers, including into the cuts and set aside for 30 minutes. Rinse the cucumbers under running water and drain well.

3 Mix together the spring onion, carrot, chives, garlic, ginger, chilli powder and fish sauce with ¼ cup water. Stuff the cucumbers with the mixture and rub the remainder on the outside. Pack tightly into a non-reactive container and stand in or out of the fridge for at least 30 minutes before serving. Scatter with a few sesame seeds to serve.

1   **STUFFED CUCUMBER KIMCHI**
2   **SPINACH NAMUL**
3   **POTATOES BRAISED IN SOY SAUCE**
4   **BEANSPROUT SOUP**

OILED GREENS

SERVES 4 AS A SHARED DISH PREPARATION TIME 5 MINS **COOKING TIME 5 MINS**

If you've always wanted to make Asian greens taste like the dish you order
in a Chinese restaurant, this is how.

INGREDIENTS

1 bunch Chinese broccoli (*gailan*)
(about 250g)

2 tbsp salt

1 tbsp vegetable oil

Oyster sauce

¼ cup oyster sauce

¼ cup Coarse Stock (page 32), Chicken
Stock (page 33) or water

¼ tsp cornflour mixed with 1 tbsp stock
or water

METHOD

1 Trim the Chinese broccoli of any dry ends and rinse
well in cold water. Cut into 10cm lengths, grouping together
the thick stalks, thin stalks and leaves separately. Split any
very thick stalks in half lengthways.

2 Bring 2 litres of water to a rolling boil and add the salt.
Add the thick stalks and boil for about a minute, then
add the thin stalks and the leaves on top. Pour over the
vegetable oil and boil for a further 2 minutes, occasionally
shaking the greens in the water with tongs or chopsticks to
coat them in the oil and to dissolve the salt. Remove from
the water and drain well.

3 For the oyster sauce, bring the oyster sauce and stock
to a simmer, then add the cornflour mixture. Stir until
thickened then remove from the heat. Serve the greens
as they are, or with some of the oyster sauce poured over
the top.

NOTES

This process can be applied to any Asian vegetable, just adjust the cooking
time accordingly.

This is a great way to cook Western vegetables as well. You can even replace
the vegetable oil with butter.

SUMMER VEGETABLES IN LIGHT SOY STOCK
Yasai no yakibitashi

SERVES 4 AS PART OF A SHARED MEAL PREPARATION TIME 15 MINS **COOKING TIME 20 MINS**

I generally don't like to use too many different kinds of vegetables in a single dish, as I find it confuses the flavours. This Japanese dish is an exception, but by keeping the vegetables separate throughout cooking, steeping and eating, they each retain their own flavours.

INGREDIENTS

2 Japanese eggplants or ½ eggplant

4 half-moon slices (about 200g) Japanese pumpkin, ½cm thick

4 cherry tomatoes

4 okra, woody ends trimmed

1 zucchini, cut into thick batons

2 thick spring onions, white and light green part only, cut into 5cm lengths

1 tsp vegetable oil

1 tbsp bonito flakes, to serve

Steeping stock

1 cup Bonito Stock (page 32)

2 tbsp sake

2 tbsp soy sauce

½ tsp grated ginger

METHOD

1 Mix the ingredients for the steeping stock together in a small saucepan and bring to a simmer, then pour the hot stock into a tray large enough to accommodate the vegetables.

2 Cut the eggplant into thick wedges and score the skin in a small cross-hatch pattern.

3 Fry the vegetables in batches in a lightly oiled frypan over medium heat, until each batch is cooked through and tender. As the vegetables are cooked, remove them from the pan and place them straight into the tray of stock. Allow to sit in the stock for at least 10 minutes.

4 Arrange the vegetables on a serving plate and pour over a few tablespoons of the stock. Place a small mound of bonito flakes on top and serve either warm or at room temperature.

NOTES

Bonito flakes are a fantastic ingredient to keep handy. They can be used as a final touch of umami for a dish like this, to make stock (page 32), or even as a seasoning in stir-fried dishes.

It's important to transfer the vegetables straight from the pan to the stock while they are still hot. As they cool even slightly they will start to absorb the flavourful liquid.

This same steeping stock can be used for any vegetables in season. Grilled asparagus and shiitake mushrooms are very good, as is spinach quickly blanched in boiling water.

SIMMERED PUMPKIN
Kabocha no nimono

SERVES 4 AS A SHARED DISH PREPARATION TIME 15 MINS **COOKING TIME 20 MINS + COOLING TIME**

There's an elegance in the relationship between ingredients and seasonings in Japanese cooking. Seasonings are used to enhance the natural flavour of ingredients, not to overpower them. The goal of a dish like this is not to make the pumpkin taste like soy sauce, or bonito flakes, or sake. It is just to make the pumpkin taste like the most flavourful version of itself.

INGREDIENTS

500g *kabocha* or Japanese pumpkin, seeds removed

2 cups Bonito Stock (page 32)

1 tsp sugar

1 tbsp soy sauce

1 tbsp sake

1 tbsp mirin

METHOD

1   Cut the pumpkin into 7cm chunks, bevel the sharp edges and remove most of the rind of the pumpkin from each piece with a sharp knife (do not remove the rind completely). Place the pumpkin in a small saucepan with the remaining ingredients and bring to the boil. Reduce the heat to a simmer and cover with a drop lid or a cartouche of baking paper. Simmer for 12 minutes, or until the pumpkin is just tender. (Test by piercing with a skewer. The skewer should pass through the pumpkin easily.)

2   Remove the drop lid and simmer for a further 5 minutes to reduce the liquid a little more, then turn off the heat and allow to cool. Serve at room temperature or reheat to serve.

NOTES

Like the daikon in the Chicken and Vegetable Nimono (page 58), bevelling the edges of the pumpkin is both for presentation and to preserve the clarity and texture of the simmering stock. It's very important.

While pumpkin rind softens and is quite delicious, too much of it will spoil the texture of each piece of pumpkin. I tend to leave just a little on each piece for flavour, texture and appearance.

Japanese stewed dishes (*nimono*) like this aren't meant to be swimming in liquid, but they shouldn't be dry either. Reduce the liquid as much as you can in the saucepan without overcooking the vegetables, and when transferring the pumpkin to the bowl add enough to keep the pumpkin moist and dressed with the flavourful liquid, like a thin sauce.

VEGETABLE KAKIAGE

SERVES 2 PREPARATION TIME 15 MINS **COOKING TIME 10 MINS**

These light tempura fritters are easier to make than they look, and are an impressive variation on ordinary tempura. Once you're comfortable with the basics of tempura on page 54, perhaps give this a try. Onions and carrots are the most simple type of *kakiage*, but they're also great made with any mixture of vegetables or seafood. Try adding burdock root, green beans, corn, chopped prawns, scallops or fresh herbs.

INGREDIENTS

2 litres vegetable oil, for deep-frying

2 large brown onions, peeled and thinly sliced

1 large carrot, cut into matchsticks

2 thick spring onions, finely sliced

1 cup tempura batter (page 54)

Fine salt, to serve

Tentsuyu (dipping sauce for tempura), to serve (page 54)

METHOD

1 Heat the oil to 165°C in a deep frypan or saucepan.

2 Combine the onions, carrots and spring onions with the tempura batter and toss to coat. With a pair of chopsticks take a generous amount of the mixture and lower it into the oil. Use the chopsticks to mould the frying mixture into a disc shape.

3 Skim off any batter bits and fry the *kakiage* for 3 minutes, or until lightly golden, then flip the disc and cook for a further 2 minutes. Drain on a wire rack. Repeat for the remaining mixture. Serve the *kakiage* with salt or with Tentsuyu.

NOTES

I prefer these only very lightly bound with tempura batter, but they are more fragile the less batter you use. If this is your first time making *kakiage*, perhaps add a little more batter to hold everything together.

As with ordinary tempura, the batter will crisp after it comes out of the oil. Don't be disappointed if your *kakiage* look a bit limp in the oil, they will crisp once drained.

You can serve the *kakiage* just as they are, or on top of a bowl of rice or even with some Cold Udon Noodles (page 111) or soba noodles.

LESSON 7
SEAFOOD

Asian cuisines prize seafood above almost anything else. Whole fish are eaten to mark special milestones, and expensive shellfish are served almost as status symbols in many countries. In Japan, the very best tuna can sell for more than a million dollars for a single fish.

Even today, many discerning Chinese restaurants keep tanks of live fish, crabs, lobsters and abalone to ensure these treasured ingredients are at their freshest and best. I grew up running around these kinds of restaurants with my siblings and family friends, while the adults chatted after dinner. We would press our noses up to the glass and coo with wonder when a bow-tied waiter would pull a fish or lobster out of a tank for someone's birthday, anniversary or other special occasion. I didn't know it back then, but it was the start of a food education.

But seafood in Asian cookery is not just fine dining. Mostly seafood is eaten not as a treat or event, but as a healthy and delicious daily staple.

When I lived in Japan I was astounded by the connection that the people had to seafood in everyday life. An average person on the street could tell you which fish were in season at different times of the year and the best ways to cook them, and even which parts of Japan specialised in particular local species. Supermarkets stocked a huge variety of fish and shellfish, and people cooked and ate dozens of different seafood dishes both at home and in restaurants.

If you don't know a lot about seafood, it can be easy to get stuck in a rut of buying the same varieties of fish again and again. Expanding the range of seafood you cook with and eat is a simple way to bring a greater range of dishes to your kitchen. With meat and poultry there are relatively few different kinds to choose from, but with seafood there are hundreds of different species.

CHOOSING SEAFOOD

When buying seafood, fresh is best. Whole fish should have clear, bright eyes and look shiny and even feel a little slippery. Fillets should look wet and dense, without cracks or big gaps in the flesh. Both whole fish and fillets should smell fresh and like seawater. If a fish smells fishy or has an unpleasant odour, it's past its best.

When buying shellfish, its weight is the best guide of both quality and freshness. A large oyster, crab or lobster that feels light may not contain much meat. Prawns should not have any black discolouration in their heads.

A simple way to explore seafood and ensure you're choosing the best kinds is to find a fishmonger that you trust and follow their advice. A good fishmonger will be able to tell you what's in season, what's at its best on any particular day, and give you advice on what fish to choose for a particular style of cooking.

PREPARING A MUD CRAB

1   Place the crab in the freezer for up to 30 minutes until it goes to sleep and stops moving.

2   Separate the carapace (upper shell) from the body and legs with your hands. Scrape out any yellow or greenish paste from the body of the crab (called 'miso', 'mustard' or 'tomalley') and reserve it.

3   Turn the crab over and remove the flap at the rear. On a male crab the flap is triangular, on a female it is larger and more rounded. If there is any roe under the flap of a female crab, reserve it. With your fingers pull away the gills and discard them.

4   Cut the crab in half from front to back.

5   Break off the claws.

6   Crack them with the back of a knife.

7   Divide each half of the crab in half again.

8   This leaves you with two legs on each piece.

BLACK PEPPER AND CARAMEL BRAISED FISH

Ca kho to

SERVES 4 PREPARATION TIME 15 MINS + COOLING TIME **COOKING TIME 30 MINS**

In Vietnamese cuisine it's important to know how to manage sweetness. The dark caramel used in this dish is taken to the bitter end of the caramelisation of sugar, then balanced with fish sauce and delicate coconut water for a taste that is fresh and just slightly sweet rather than cloying.

INGREDIENTS

500g basa or other white fish fillets, skin removed

½ tsp salt

2 tbsp peanut oil

4 eschalots or 1 large brown onion, peeled and sliced

2 tbsp fish sauce

1 cup coconut water or 1 cup water and ½ tsp sugar

3 thick spring onions, trimmed and sliced into 5cm lengths

1 large red chilli, sliced diagonally

Ground black pepper, to serve

Cooked rice, to serve

Vietnamese caramel sauce (*nuoc mau*)

1 cup sugar

¼ cup cold water

½ cup boiling water

METHOD

1   To make the caramel sauce, mix the sugar and cold water in a small saucepan and heat over medium heat for about 10 minutes, swirling the pot occasionally (do not stir with a spoon). Watch the sugar carefully as it starts to change colour and keep a kettle of hot water handy. When the caramel reaches a deep golden brown, add the hot water (be careful, as the hot caramel may spit) and stir to dissolve the caramel to a thick sauce. Allow to cool to room temperature.

2   Rub the fish with salt and rinse well under running water, then pat dry with paper towel. Cut each fillet into thirds. Heat the oil in a claypot or lidded frypan and fry the eschalots for a few minutes until softened. Add ¼ cup of the caramel sauce, the fish sauce, and coconut water and boil, uncovered, until the volume is reduced by half. Add the fish, spring onion and chilli and turn to coat in the sauce. Partially cover the pot and simmer for 4 minutes, or until the fish is cooked through. Grind over plenty of black pepper and serve with rice.

NOTES

The caramel sauce will keep in a jar in the fridge indefinitely.

Unsweetened coconut water has become popular recently as a health drink. It is available from supermarkets, Asian grocers and health food shops.

While this recipe uses delicate and easily available basa fillets, in Vietnam it is more commonly made with cutlets of catfish on the bone. You could also use another firm, white fish such as ling, or even prawns, chicken or pork. Just adjust the cooking time accordingly.

FISH BALL NOODLE SOUP

SERVES 4 PREPARATION TIME 15 MINS **COOKING TIME 20 MINS**

Fish ball noodle soup has been one of my favourite dishes since childhood. My grandmother would make it for me when I was feeling a bit peckish as it just uses ingredients that we would consider staples in our house. Even today I still keep fish balls in my freezer in case the mood strikes.

INGREDIENTS

20 fish balls

1kg fresh flat rice noodles

2 cups beansprouts

½ cup fried eschalots, to serve

½ cup finely sliced thin spring onions, to serve

½ cup chopped coriander, to serve

Ground white pepper, to serve

Chillies in Soy Sauce (page 29), to serve

Soup stock

1 tbsp vegetable oil

1cm ginger, sliced and bruised

3 cloves garlic, peeled and finely chopped

2 litres Chicken Stock (page 33), or Anchovy Stock (page 33)

2 thick spring onions, roots and dark green ends trimmed and discarded

1½ tsp salt

1 tsp soy sauce

METHOD

1   For the soup stock, place all the ingredients in a large pot, bring to a low simmer and simmer for 10 minutes. Pick out the spring onions and ginger and discard.

2   Add the fish balls to the pot, return to a simmer and simmer for 5 minutes, or until the fish balls are puffed and cooked through.

3   Bring a separate large pot of water to the boil, place one-quarter of the noodles and a handful of beansprouts in a sieve and lower the sieve into the boiling water for 1 minute, until the noodles are cooked and the beansprouts softened. Drain well, and place the noodles in a bowl. Repeat for the remaining noodles and beansprouts.

4   Ladle the soup stock and fish balls into each of the bowls, top with the fried eschalots, spring onions and coriander and sprinkle with ground white pepper. Serve with the Chillies in Soy Sauce.

NOTES

Fish balls are relatively simple to make by just pounding together white fish with a few seasonings and a touch of oil, but for your first time making this soup, I recommend buying pre-made fish balls. There are many different varieties available from Asian grocers and some supermarkets.

If you want to add more vegetables to this dish, a handful of iceberg lettuce (shredded finely or torn into chunks) is great cooked in clear soup.

Whenever you cook noodles for a clear soup, cook them in a separate pot of unsalted water as cooking them in the soup will turn the soup cloudy. You could also add a dash of alcohol (Shaoxing wine, sake or mirin) to the soup stock to give more depth to the flavour.

WHITE FISH TERIYAKI
Buri no teriyaki

SERVES 2 PREPARATION TIME 10 MINS **COOKING TIME 15 MINS**

Teriyaki chicken may be a favourite in the West, but in Japan the teriyaki style of cooking is almost always used for white fish. It's a very popular dish in Japanese home cooking.

INGREDIENTS

1 tsp vegetable oil

2 thick spring onions, white and light green part cut into 5cm pieces

2 fillets ling or kingfish, around 150g each

Teriyaki glaze
(makes approximately 650ml)

200ml mirin

200ml sake

60g sugar

250ml soy sauce

METHOD

1   For the teriyaki glaze, mix all the ingredients together in a small saucepan and stir over medium heat just until the sugar dissolves. Transfer to a clean jar or bottle.

2   Heat a frypan over medium heat and add the oil. Fry the spring onions for a few minutes until lightly browned and softened. Remove from the frypan. Add the fish fillets and fry for about 2 minutes on each side until lightly browned, then add ¼ cup of the teriyaki glaze. Continue to fry, turning the fish through the glaze every minute until the glaze is thick, glossy, coating the fish, and the fish is just cooked through. This will depend on the thickness of the fillets, but it should only take a few minutes. You can add a little more teriyaki glaze if you want a stronger flavour. Transfer the fish from the pan to a plate with the spring onions, and pour over any thick glaze remaining in the pan to serve.

NOTES

The term *teriyaki* roughly translates to 'glazed grill' in Japanese, and it should be a light, glossy glaze over whatever you cook with it.

Homemade teriyaki glaze is something I always keep in my pantry. The recipe given here makes a volume that will fit in an empty wine or soy sauce bottle. It will keep in the pantry indefinitely.

For teriyaki chicken, just follow the same process, replacing the fish with sliced chicken thigh fillets dusted with a little cornflour.

MARINATED TUNA RICE BOWL
Magurozuke don

SERVES 4 PREPARATION TIME 20 MINS + 15 MINS MARINATING TIME **COOKING TIME 5 MINS**

Raw fish in Japanese cuisine is not only served as sashimi. While the fish may be the main focus in this tuna rice bowl, the spring onion, perilla, nori, sesame and wasabi that come along with it are more than just garnishes, they are the key to turning a few slices of good-quality fish into a complete and balanced meal.

INGREDIENTS

400g sashimi-grade tuna

8 cups cooked short-grain rice, warm

4 thin spring onions, trimmed and finely sliced, to serve

1 tbsp toasted sesame seeds, to serve

4 perilla (*shiso*) leaves (optional), to serve

1 sheet nori, finely shredded, to serve

1 tsp wasabi, to serve

Marinade

3 tbsp sake

2 tbsp mirin

3 tbsp soy sauce

METHOD

1   To make the marinade, bring the sake and mirin to the boil in a small saucepan. Boil for 1 minute then remove from the heat, add the soy sauce, pour the sauce into a tray and allow to cool to room temperature.

2   Slice the tuna as you like and place the slices in the marinade. Marinate for 15 minutes.

3   Divide the rice among four deep bowls. Scatter the rice with the spring onions and a few sesame seeds, and place a perilla leaf, if using, to one side of the bowl. Arrange the marinated tuna on top of the rice and gloss the tuna with just a little of the marinade, letting it run down onto the rice. Scatter with the remaining sesame seeds, some of the nori and place a little pile of wasabi next to the tuna.

NOTES

The '*don*' in the Japanese name for this dish is short for *donburi*, meaning 'rice bowl'. *Donburi* are popular one-bowl meals in Japan consisting of a bowl of warm, cooked rice with various toppings. Try the glazed pork version on page 206.

Changing how you cut the tuna will give different textures in the dish. The most common cut is in thin, sashimi-style square cut slices as shown on page 53, but you could try it in thicker slices, cubes or even roughly minced.

You can make this *donburi* with any sashimi-grade fish, or even a mixture of raw seafood.

MISO-CURED COD
Saikyo yaki

SERVES 4 PREPARATION TIME 5 MINS + OVERNIGHT MARINATING **COOKING TIME 7 MINS**

Miso is a versatile ingredient that can be used for more than just soup. In this dish, the miso lightly cures the fish for a complex sweet and umami flavour.

INGREDIENTS

200g white miso

2 tbsp mirin

1 tbsp sake

500g cod or blue-eye trevalla fillets, cleaned and scaled (if necessary)

Lemon or lime cheeks, to serve

METHOD

1 Mix the miso, mirin and sake together to form a smooth paste. Spread a little of the miso mixture over the base of a non-reactive bowl or tray and place the fish fillets on top. Cover the fish with the remaining miso mixture. Cover with plastic wrap directly onto the surface of the miso and refrigerate overnight.

2 Heat your overhead grill to medium-high. With a spatula, scrape away as much of the miso from the fish as you can. Place the fish on an oiled baking tray and grill for about 7 minutes, adjusting the time depending on the thickness of the fillets. You don't need to turn the fish. Serve with a cheek of lemon or lime.

NOTES

Known as *saikyo yaki*, this method of curing in miso can be used for many different ingredients. Firm fish such as salmon or ling work well, as do chicken thighs or even large pieces of pork belly.

Scraping away the miso is important as this dish shouldn't taste strongly of miso. It is a curing process, not a marinade. Look for the lightly burnished colour on the edge of the fish when grilling. This is where the sweetness of the miso cure is helping caramelise the fish.

It's best to use a lighter coloured miso for this dish – dark misos will have a stronger flavour that may overpower the fish.

SALT-GRILLED SALMON
Shioyaki

SERVES 4 PREPARATION TIME 5 MINS **COOKING TIME 10 MINS**

Salt-grilled fish is a staple of Japanese cuisine, and this simple technique can be used with fillets, cutlets, slices or even whole fish of many different varieties. Japanese home cooks use purpose-specific fish grills that simulate the effect of cooking over open coals, but here are two different methods to achieve the same result without needing any special equipment.

INGREDIENTS

10cm of a medium-sized daikon, peeled

600g salmon fillets, scaled

1 tsp fine salt

1 tsp vegetable oil

Lemon slices, to serve

½ tsp soy sauce, to serve

NOTES

Whenever something sticks to a frypan it's usually that the pan wasn't hot enough at the beginning of cooking. If frying, make sure the pan is very hot before adding the fish to avoid it sticking to the pan. This doesn't mean just cooking over high heat. A frypan left over medium heat will get just as hot as it would over high heat. It just might take a little longer.

White globules of protein will form on the surface of the salmon when it is overcooked. If you see them, the fish will have a drier texture. There's nothing wrong with that. Some in Japan even prefer it.

In Japan a small piece of fish grilled like this is often served with a few pickles, a bowl of rice and some miso soup for a delicious breakfast.

METHOD

1 Grate the daikon radish on a Japanese grater or the finest holes of a box grater to produce about a cup of grated daikon. Lightly squeeze and discard the excess bitter liquid. Set aside.

2 Pat the fish dry with paper towel and season all over with salt, applying most of the salt to the skin.

3 *To grill*: Heat your overhead grill to medium-high. Place a piece of foil on a baking tray and rub with the oil. Place the fish skin-side down on the foil and grill for 7–10 minutes, or until cooked through. When pressed on the sides the fish should feel just firm, but not bouncy or tough. Remove from the oven and separate the fish from the skin using a spatula, leaving the skin stuck to the foil. If you want to serve the skin, scrape off any fat and dark-brown bloodline and discard. Return the skin to the grill under high heat for 3 minutes, or until it blisters. Remove from the foil and leave aside for a minute to crisp. Serve the crispy skin with the salmon.

Fry: Heat a frypan over medium heat until very hot, then add the oil. Place the fish fillets skin-side down and press the fillets firmly for around 30 seconds to keep the skin in contact with the pan. Cook for about 4 minutes on the skin side, then flip and cook for about 3 minutes until the fish is cooked through.

4 Place a mound of grated daikon on a slice of lemon and drizzle a little soy sauce on top. Serve the fish with the daikon.

SAMBAL SQUID

SERVES 4 PREPARATION TIME 10 MINS **COOKING TIME 20 MINS**

Many Asian dishes preserve the delicate flavour of seafood by matching it with light seasonings, but this Malaysian favourite is not one of those. The strongly flavoured sambal may be spicy, but if balanced well it won't overpower the flavour of the seafood.

INGREDIENTS

1 tbsp tamarind pulp, loosened in ¼ cup hot water

¼ cup vegetable oil

1 medium onion, peeled and thinly sliced

2 tsp chopped palm sugar, or 1½ tsp white sugar

½ tsp salt

2 tomatoes, cut into wedges

500g squid, cleaned and cut into rings

Lime wedges, to serve

Rempah

6 eschalots, or 2 small onions, peeled and sliced

5 large red chillies

3 bird's-eye chillies

3 cloves garlic, peeled

2 tsp *belacan* (shrimp paste)

4 candlenuts, macadamia nuts or cashews (optional)

METHOD

1 Mix the tamarind pulp with the ¼ cup hot water, rubbing through with your fingers or a spoon to loosen the seeds from the pulp, pass through a sieve and discard the seeds, reserving the thick tamarind water.

2 Place the ingredients for the *rempah* in a blender or food processor and blend to a fine paste.

3 Heat a wok or lidded frypan over medium heat and add the oil. Add the *rempah* and fry for about 5 minutes, stirring regularly until fragrant and the oil separates from the solids. Add the onion, tamarind water, palm sugar or sugar, salt and tomatoes to the pan and bring to a simmer. Simmer, covered, for 5–10 minutes, or until the tomatoes and onions have softened. Add the squid and simmer for 2 minutes, or just until the squid is tender. Taste and adjust for seasoning. Serve with lime wedges.

NOTES

Matching strong flavours with seafood is perfectly fine, and many seafoods work well with spicy and sour-savoury flavour combinations. Just keep your eye on the sweet flavours. A dish that is too sugary will overshadow seafood's delicate sweetness.

This sambal is great with prawns or oily fish, and is ideal for eating with coconut rice in the classic Malaysian *nasi lemak*.

Candlenut is an oily nut used in Malaysian and Indonesian cuisines to give a slightly thick and creamy texture to sauces, in the same way cashews may be used in a *korma* in Indian cuisine. Macadamia nuts are a good substitute if you can't find candlenuts in your local Asian grocer.

LESSON 8
POULTRY

In the past many Asian families kept poultry both as a source of eggs and for meat. When I was young I would daily collect the chicken and duck eggs from our small suburban coop, and once in a while my grandmother would kill one of the birds for a meal.

CHOOSING CHICKEN

Chicken stock is a vital part of so many world cuisines, so it's strange that many people believe chicken only has a very mild flavour. Well-raised and well-cooked chicken is strongly flavoured and delicious.

When choosing chicken, it's important to consider its breed, age and growing conditions. Different breeds of chicken have different flavours, and it's common throughout Asia to have chickens sold by breed. In Australia, quarantine laws mean our access to different breeds of chicken is limited, but the age and growing conditions of birds are still important.

As a rule, older birds will be tougher and have more flavour, while younger birds will be more tender and milder. While most chickens sold for eating will be young birds, some butchers, specialist poultry shops and Asian grocers will sell older chickens. Older chickens make excellent stocks, but in Asian cuisines they are often eaten for meat as well and enjoyed for their strong flavour and meaty texture.

With regard to growing conditions, free-range or pasture-raised birds that have freedom to walk around and exercise are the obvious choice over birds that are intensively farmed. This is both for ethical reasons regarding the animal's welfare, and because birds that are able to move around have more flavour than those that do not.

DARK MEAT VS LIGHT MEAT

In Asian cookery, the dark meat of poultry is favoured over the light meat for its flavour and juicy texture. In chicken, the dark meat is the meat of the neck, thigh, and drumstick, while the white meat is the wing and breast. The difference is easily explained by the physiology of the bird.

Dark meat areas are muscles that are used by the animal for prolonged activity, as the darker colouring is caused by higher levels of oxygen-carrying protein known as myoglobin. A chicken spends a lot of time walking around and pecking the ground, resulting in dark meat in the legs and neck. In contrast, it only flies in short bursts, requiring a different kind of muscle comprising the white meat of the wings and breasts. Ducks fly long distances, which is why the wing and breast meat from ducks is dark.

Dark meat contains more fat than light meat, which gives the meat more flavour and keeps it moist.

DON'T OVERCOOK POULTRY

The key to delicious poultry is to keep it as juicy as possible, and the easiest way to ensure poultry remains juicy is to cook it well. Overcooking is a common mistake when preparing poultry, driven by a fear of undercooking it.

Our approach to cooking poultry is as much cultural as it is scientific. In Japan eating raw chicken is fairly common, but duck is usually cooked to well done. In the West we are generally fine with duck served still pink, but would baulk at chicken cooked to the same standard. In China and much of Southeast Asia, all poultry is traditionally cooked through (and all meats are, too, for that matter).

I'm certainly not suggesting everyone must start eating raw chicken or medium-rare duck, but there is a big difference between meat or poultry that is well-cooked through and that which is overcooked.

As meat and poultry cook, the fibres of the muscles tighten, causing it to shrink. With poultry we generally cook whole muscles (like a whole breast or whole thigh), which means that the fibres are longer than those of, say, a steak that has been sliced across the grain. As the long fibres shrink, they physically squeeze moisture from the muscle like squeezing water from a sponge. That moisture is crucial for both flavour and texture.

RESIDUAL HEAT

To cook poultry (or meat) to the correct point without overcooking, it's important to understand the concept of residual heat.

We cook by applying heat to the outside of ingredients, and wait for that heat to be conducted to the inside. For example, we heat the outside of a piece of chicken, and then the outside of the chicken transfers that heat to the inside of the chicken. This is important because it means that even after we remove the piece of chicken from our heat source (like taking it out of a pan), the outside of the chicken will continue to conduct heat to the inside and it will continue to cook. If we cook the piece of chicken in the pan to exactly how we want it, by the time we come to eat it, it will be overcooked.

To avoid overcooking, it is therefore important to cook an ingredient to a point just before the level of doneness we would like, and then rest it to allow it to cook completely.

To test whether a piece of food is done, the best way to do so without resorting to thermometers is by pressing it with your fingers. As meat and poultry cook, they will become more firm. Just keep pressing the piece of food with your fingers and feel how it changes. With practice, you will be able to tell how something is cooked just by the feel of it.

RESTING

Understanding residual heat goes hand-in-hand with the concept of resting. Resting is vital to good cookery. I rest just about everything I cook – stir-fried dishes, steaks, and even whole roasted chickens or joints of meat. They all benefit from a bit of resting time.

Resting allows flavourful juices within the meat to be redistributed, resulting in a tastier and juicier product. It's often said that the rule of thumb is that meat and poultry should be rested for around half the time it took to cook. This is not a bad rule, but the amount of resting time is really more dependent on the size of the piece cooked rather than the time it takes to cook. The rule works in many cases because larger pieces of meat or poultry take longer to cook, but it does have its limitations.

Thinly sliced chicken in a wok-fried dish may only need to be rested for a minute or so regardless of how long it was fried for, but a whole thigh fillet should rest for around 5 minutes, whether it was cooked for 6 minutes or 10. A whole chicken roasted for an hour or more would only need to be rested for around 15 minutes as it is cooked on the bone, keeping it moist.

You don't need to be afraid of your food going cold while it is resting. Meat and poultry hold heat very well. You just need to prevent external factors cooling the meat down.

When I rest meat or poultry, I heat a small tray or plate in the oven or on a stove until it is just warm to the touch. This stops the chill of the plate from cooling the meat. I place the food on the tray or plate and put it in a draught-free place, or loosely cover it with foil to stop any breeze from evaporating moisture and cooling the meat further. The result is perfectly cooked, warm, and tender food that retains its natural juices.

COOKING ON THE BONE

Bones provide a lot of flavour, which is why they're so useful for stocks. That same effect applies to cooking on the bone. When poultry or meat is cooked on the bone, the bones provide flavour both to the meat and to any liquid it is cooked in. Try cooking dishes like Steamed Ginger Chicken (page 10) using chicken pieces on the bone. Or contrast the strong flavour of Nyonya Chicken Stew (page 18) or Korean Braised Chilli Chicken (page 14) with a whole chopped chicken compared with pieces of thigh fillets. The difference is striking.

For poultry, the bone has an additional effect of allowing the muscles to keep their structure. When attached to the bone, the meat of poultry is kept stretched along the length of the bone, meaning that the muscle fibres don't contract as much, and don't squeeze out as much of the juices. The result is a much juicier, more flavourful and tender bird. Chicken breast and wing are both white meat, but when cooked close to the bone the meat of the wing is much more flavourful than the breast.

Cook poultry on the bone whenever you can, whether it's in pieces or as a whole bird.

BUYING WHOLE BIRDS

It makes a lot of sense to buy whole birds rather than trays of breast or thigh fillets. Buying whole birds is cheaper, provides you with a source of bones for stock, gives you a greater variety in what you eat, and also helps you to be more creative in the kitchen.

I usually buy one or two whole chickens per week, then spend a few minutes deboning one (or both) to make stock from the bones as well as yielding a variety of cuts of chicken that I can use over the following few days.

I think deboning a chicken is a fundamental skill all cooks should learn. Simply breaking a whole chicken down to Marylands, breast fillets, wings and a carcass should really take only a few seconds if you know what you're doing (Steps 1–4 on page 164), but in Asian cooking it's common to go a step further to completely remove the bones from the leg, providing an extended leg fillet that can be cooked just as it is for a dish like Crackling Chicken Steak (page 171), or cut up for wok-fried dishes or dishes like Red Pepper Chicken (page 179). The breasts can also be used for wok-fried dishes or for quick-cooking in dishes like Chicken, Coconut and Galangal Soup (page 180). Just having the different cuts of chicken ready to use makes daily cooking a more varied task than if you just buy the same cuts over and over again. It forces you to think about what you're cooking, rather than shopping, cooking and eating on auto-pilot.

In the next few pages there are a couple of important skills you should know when dealing with whole poultry – cutting up whole birds both raw and cooked.

The technique for deboning a whole raw bird is fairly simple, but just takes a little practice. The same goes for chopping a chicken or duck 'Chinese-style'. You may not get it right the first time but please persevere. Knowing how to do these two things will improve the way you cook and eat poultry for the rest of your life.

DEBONING A RAW CHICKEN

The major difference between deboning a chicken in an Asian style from a Western style is that the thigh and drumstick remain attached as one large extended fillet. This is useful as the thigh and drumstick meat can be used for the same purpose. Most of this can be done with a boning knife instead of a cleaver if you prefer, but you will still need a cleaver for a few of the steps.

1   Hold the chicken by the legs and give it a little shake to loosen the hip joints. Starting at the drumstick of the chicken, cut through the space between the leg and the body to the hip joint, dislocate the leg from the body and slide the knife around the oyster, removing the leg completely from the body. Repeat with the other leg.

2   Remove both wings from the body by cutting through the underside of the wing between the wing and the breast, keeping a bit of the breast meat with the wing. You should be cutting through the cartilage of the joints and not bone.

3   Turn the bird so that the breasts are facing you. Cut down either side of the keel bone of the chicken and remove the breasts. Separate the tenderloins from each breast if you prefer.

4   Cutting through the joints, separate each wing into three parts: the drumette, winglet and wing tip.

5   To debone the legs completely, cut an L-shape in the underside of the leg to the bone, following the line of the bone.

6   Loosen the bone from the meat at the hip joint and, holding the bone against the cutting board with the cleaver, pull the thigh meat away from the bone.

7   At the ankle of the drumstick, break the bone with a sharp tap of the cleaver. Use the cleaver to press the bone against the cutting board, and holding the drumstick by the ankle, pull the drumstick meat away from the bone to the knee joint.

8   With short cuts of the knife, work the meat away from the knee joint to completely remove the bone. Cut the ankle from the extended drumstick and thigh fillet.

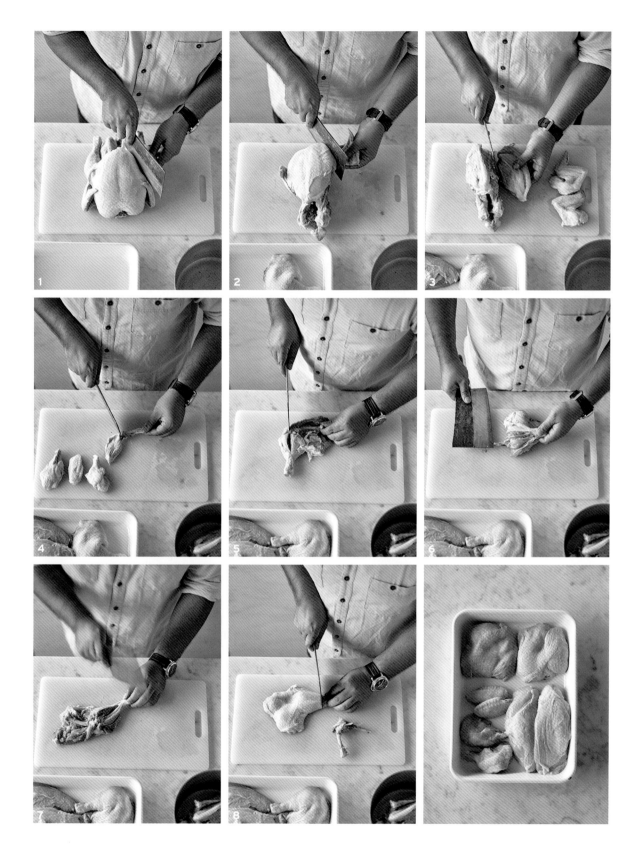

CHOPPING COOKED POULTRY 'CHINESE-STYLE'

The Chinese style of chopping a cooked bird (whether it is a duck or chicken) can be difficult to get the hang of at first, but it's really not all that hard. The idea is that the bird is cut into small pieces with its bones, so that it is easy to share and to eat with chopsticks. You'll need a heavy cleaver.

1   Take a well-rested cooked chicken or duck. With a heavy cleaver, divide the bird entirely in half from front to back, through the backbone and breastbone.

2   With one half of the bird, make a small cut under the wing shoulder joint and chop through the 'heel' of the breast to remove the wing.

3   Remove the drumstick by cutting under the drumstick and chopping through the thigh bone close to the joint of the drumstick. From the half of the chicken you should now be left with a wing (including a small part of the breast), a drumstick (with a small part of the thigh), and the breast and thigh fillets remaining on the half-carcass.

4   Divide the half-carcass lengthways with the breast on one side and the thigh on the other.

5   Pull the breast meat away from the tenderloin and carcass.

6   Chop the tenderloin and the attached bones into 1–2cm slices and transfer to a serving plate. Cut the breast meat across the grain into slices of the same width and transfer to the serving plate.

7   Chop the thigh meat through the bone into slices of the same width and transfer to the serving plate.

8   Chop the drumstick and wing into pieces and place on the serving plate as well.

KHMER KROM BARBECUE CHICKEN

SERVES 4 PREPARATION TIME 15 MINS + 1 HOUR MARINATING **COOKING TIME 1 HOUR**

This delicious method of cooking a chicken on a barbecue comes from the south of Vietnam and Cambodia. The chicken slowly steams in its marinade, resulting in a tender and flavourful bird that's then unwrapped and browned for a delicious barbecue flavour.

INGREDIENTS

2 thick spring onions, trimmed and finely chopped

3 cloves garlic, peeled and minced

1 tbsp honey

1 tsp sugar

½ tsp salt

3 tbsp fish sauce

1 tsp ground black pepper

1 tsp turmeric powder

Juice of 1 lime (about 50ml)

3 kaffir lime leaves, finely sliced

2 tbsp vegetable oil, plus 2 extra tablespoons for basting

1 whole chicken (about 1.7kg)

2 large banana leaves (optional)

METHOD

1 Combine all the ingredients except the chicken and banana leaves in a bowl to make the marinade.

2 With a cleaver, heavy knife or poultry shears, cut down either side of the backbone of the chicken and remove it. Press firmly down on the breast of the bird to flatten it.

3 Lay the banana leaves in a cross pattern. Rub the marinade all over the chicken and place in the centre of the cross. Wrap the chicken in the banana leaves to completely enclose the bird. Wrap the package again in foil. This will help keep the banana leaves sealed during cooking. If you don't have banana leaves you can use a double layer of foil instead.

4 Set the package of chicken aside for at least 1 hour to marinate, but preferably overnight. If marinating overnight, stand the chicken for 1 hour out of the fridge to return to room temperature before cooking.

5 Heat a barbecue grill over medium heat. Place the package of chicken on the grill and grill for 45 minutes, turning every 10 minutes. Carefully unwrap the chicken and return to the grill for a further 10 minutes, turning regularly until nicely charred. Rest the chicken for 10 minutes before serving.

NOTES

You can also cook this in the oven. Bake the package in a preheated 190°C oven for 1 hour, then open the top of the package and grill the skin side of the chicken under an overhead grill for 10–15 minutes until browned and crisp.

This is a great dish to bring along to a barbecue. Marinate and wrap the chicken in advance, then bring the wrapped package along with you to cook.

CRACKLING CHICKEN STEAK

SERVES 2 COOKING TIME 10 MINS

This Japanese-style chicken steak with crisp skin is one of my favourite dishes and it's proof that, in the kitchen, technique is king. If you have the skill to debone a chicken (pages 164-165) and cook it just right, delicious food never needs to be complicated.

INGREDIENTS

1 chicken thigh fillet extended with the drumstick attached, skin-on and deboned (see pages 164-165)

2 tsp vegetable oil, for cooking

Good-quality sea salt, to season

1 tsp *yuzu kosho* or wasabi, to serve

METHOD

1   Take the chicken out of the fridge about 30 minutes before cooking to bring it to room temperature. When ready to cook, heat a charcoal barbecue, heavy frypan or grill pan over medium heat until very hot. Brush the grill or pan with a small amount of oil, season the skin of the chicken liberally with salt, and cook skin-down for about 3 minutes. Season the meat side of the chicken while this is happening. Flip the chicken and cook for about 2 minutes on the flesh side, then flip the chicken every minute or so for a few minutes until nearly cooked through. Check how the chicken is cooking by pressing into the surface with your fingers. As the chicken cooks it will become more firm. Remove the chicken when it is about 85 per cent cooked through. It may take some trial and error to know what this feels like, but it will come with practice.

2   Rest the chicken, skin-side up, in a draught-free place for 5 minutes, then slice it into thick slices and serve with a little of the *yuzu kosho* or wasabi. The inside of the chicken should have a very slight blush of pink right in the centre with well-browned edges and golden crackling on top.

NOTES

Yuzu kosho is a delicious Japanese condiment made from green chilli lightly fermented and cured with salt and the rind of *yuzu*, a kind of Japanese citrus. It's available from Japanese grocers.

Cooking over charcoal gives grilled meat and poultry an earthy, almost smoky flavour that I absolutely love. Heating coals is time-consuming, and so most of the times I make this dish I do it on a cast-iron grill pan on my stove. Once in a while, however, I break out the charcoal just to remind myself what I'm missing out on when I take shortcuts for convenience.

WHITE CUT CHICKEN

SERVES 4-6 PREPARATION TIME 10 MINS **COOKING TIME 45 MINS + COOLING TIME**

White cut chicken is a staple of Chinese cooking. There are variations on it in most regions of China and around Asia. It can be served on its own or with either of the condiments shown below.

INGREDIENTS

½ cup Shaoxing wine

2 coriander roots and stalks

3 thick spring onions, trimmed and cut into 10cm lengths

2cm ginger, peeled and cut into slices

1 tbsp salt

1 whole chicken (about 1.7kg)

Cantonese-style ginger and spring onion oil

2 tbsp grated ginger

½ tsp salt flakes

4 thin spring onions, thinly sliced

3 tbsp peanut oil

Sichuan-style hot dressing

2 tsp grated ginger

2 thick spring onions, finely chopped

1 tbsp soy sauce

2 tsp Chinkiang black vinegar

2 tsp caster sugar

1 tbsp sesame oil

2 tsp chilli oil

METHOD

1   Place the wine, coriander, spring onion, ginger and salt in a large stainless-steel pot with a capacity of about 7 litres. Rinse the chicken under running water and place it into the pot. Add cold water until the chicken is covered completely. Remove the chicken and set aside.

2   Bring the poaching liquid to the boil and lower the chicken carefully into the pot (breast-side up), making sure the cavity is full with hot poaching liquid. Return the pot to the boil, cover, reduce the heat and simmer for 10 minutes. Turn the chicken and simmer for a further 10 minutes. Remove from the heat but keep the pot covered for a further 10 minutes. Remove the chicken from the pot and place in a large bowl of iced water for 5 minutes then drain well. The chicken can be served immediately while still slightly warm, or chilled in the fridge covered with plastic wrap for at least 1 hour. Chop the chicken Chinese-style (see pages 166-167) and allow it to stand for a few minutes to warm slightly.

3   *For the ginger and spring onion oil*, pound the ginger and salt to a rough paste using a heatproof mortar and pestle. Add the spring onion and pound lightly to combine. Heat the peanut oil in a small frypan until it is smoking, then pour the hot oil over the ginger mixture and stir. Serve the cut chicken with the ginger and spring onion oil on the side.

For the Sichuan-style hot dressing, combine all the ingredients in a bowl and stir to dissolve the sugar. Pour the dressing over the chicken to serve.

NOTES

The chicken should be just cooked with a soft and gelatinous skin. When cutting through the leg bones, the marrow should still be a light pink rather than brown. The final part of cooking occurs with the heat turned off. A larger pot or thicker cast-iron pot will hold the chicken and water at a higher temperature than a smaller or thinner pot. You may need to adjust the cooking time accordingly.

CRISPY SKIN CHICKEN

SERVES 4-6 PREPARATION TIME 15 MINS + 5 HOURS DRYING TIME **COOKING TIME 20 MINS**

Since I was a kid this has been one of my favourite dishes, and it's actually quite simple to make. Deep-frying a whole chicken might be a bit daunting at first, but if you have a big enough pot it's really easy.

INGREDIENTS

1 whole chicken (about 1.7kg)

2 tbsp maltose or honey

2 tbsp rice vinegar

2 tbsp Shaoxing wine

3 tbsp hot water

About 5 litres oil, for deep-frying

Lemon slices, to serve

Five spice salt

2 tbsp salt

¼ tsp Chinese five spice powder

¼ tsp white pepper

METHOD

1   With string or poultry hooks, hang the chicken under the wings. Place the chicken in a colander over the sink and pour boiling water all over the skin of the chicken until it tightens.

2   Mix the maltose, rice vinegar, Shaoxing wine and hot water together and pour over the chicken to glaze. Reserve any glaze that drips off the chicken. Hang in a breezy spot or in front of an electric fan and dry for 1 hour.

3   Heat the reserved glaze until just warm, pour over the chicken and hang it again to dry for at least 4 hours. The skin of the chicken should look dry, glazed and thin, with the meat of the chicken taking on a dark pink or even purple colour through the skin.

4   For the five spice salt, add the salt, five spice powder and pepper to a dry frypan and fry on low-medium heat for about 3 minutes, until very dry and fragrant.

5   Heat the oil in a large saucepan to 150°C and carefully lower the chicken into the oil and fry for 12 minutes, until the chicken is cooked through and the skin is golden brown. Remove the chicken from the oil and drain well. Rest for 5 minutes in a warm place. Chop the chicken Chinese-style (pages 166-167) and serve with the five spice salt.

NOTES

If you prefer not to hang the chicken in the open, you can place it 'sitting' on a full, unopened can on a wire rack in the fridge overnight. Let the chicken come to room temperature for at least an hour before frying.

It takes a bit more effort but if you don't have a big enough pot to hold the chicken and hot oil safely, you can heat about 2 litres oil in a wok over high heat, add the chicken and continuously spoon the hot oil over the chicken as it cooks. Watch out that the skin of the chicken doesn't burn in contact with the wok.

Try the five spice salt on a Crackling Chicken Steak (page 171).

TEOCHEW BRAISED DUCK

SERVES 4–6 PREPARATION TIME 15 MINS **COOKING TIME 1½ HOURS**

Roasted duck dishes like Peking duck are among the most well-known Chinese foods, but they can be a bit intimidating if you've never cooked a whole duck before. This family-style braised recipe is a great place to start.

INGREDIENTS

2 tbsp salt

1 whole duck, neck removed

1 tbsp Chinese five spice powder

1 tbsp sesame oil

8 cloves garlic, peeled and bruised

10 slices galangal, bruised
   (or substitute ginger)

1 cup sugar

¼ cup vegetable oil

1 cup dark soy sauce

750ml water

1 small brown onion, peeled and sliced

2 star anise

2 cinnamon sticks

Garlic vinegar

2 cloves garlic, peeled and finely
   chopped

¼ cup white vinegar

1 tsp sugar

½ tsp salt

METHOD

1 Rub the salt all over the duck (inside and out) then rinse under running water. Place the duck in the sink and pour boiling water over it to tighten the skin. Rub it all over with five spice powder and sesame oil, then place 3 cloves of garlic and a few slices of galangal in the cavity. Close the duck cavity with a skewer, by threading it through the skin around the cavity like a sewing thread.

2 Heat a large wok over medium heat, add the sugar and oil and continue heating, stirring occasionally, until the sugar turns to a dark caramel.

3 Add the duck and roll it through the caramel to coat. Add the dark soy sauce, water, onion, star anise, cinnamon sticks and remaining garlic and galangal and bring to a simmer, repeatedly basting the duck with the liquid. Cover and simmer for 1 hour, continuing to spoon the liquid over the duck occasionally and turning the duck halfway through cooking.

4 For the garlic vinegar, mix together all the ingredients.

5 Remove the duck from the liquid and rest for 20 minutes. Chop the duck as shown on pages 166–167. Serve with a little of the braising liquid and the garlic vinegar on the side.

NOTES

I always think that the meaty, slightly metallic taste of duck needs to be balanced with a little sweetness. It's why it goes so well with hoisin sauce for Peking duck pancakes, and with lychees in a Thai red curry.

One of the things I am most grateful to my family for is being taught to appreciate food. At almost every meal my dad would tell us kids, 'manman chi'. It's a Chinese expression which literally translates to 'eat slowly' but which really means 'take time to enjoy the meal'. Of all the things we rush through in our lives, eating shouldn't be one of them.

RED PEPPER CHICKEN
Dak galbi

SERVES 4 PREPARATION TIME 20 MINS **COOKING TIME 25 MINS**

Cooking at the table is a big part of Asian cooking. It's common across all Asian cultures – Chinese steamboat, Japanese *nabe* and all kinds of Korean grilled dishes are best when made by diners cooking on a portable stove in the centre of the table. This hot chicken dish originated in Chuncheon but is now hugely popular throughout Korea and around the world.

INGREDIENTS

600g chicken thigh fillets, cut into 4cm pieces

½ tsp sesame oil

¼ head cabbage, cut into large chunks

1 large brown onion, peeled and thickly sliced

1 small carrot, peeled and thinly sliced in rounds

1 large green chilli, sliced diagonally

1 small sweet potato, peeled and thinly sliced in rounds

300g Korean rice cakes (*tteok*), cut into 5cm lengths

8 Korean sesame leaves (perilla), thickly sliced

Sauce

2 tbsp Korean chilli powder (*gochugaru*)

1 tbsp sugar

2 tbsp soy sauce

1 tbsp sesame oil

1 tbsp Korean corn syrup (*mul yut*) or honey

3 tbsp Korean chilli paste (*gochujang*)

5 cloves garlic, peeled and minced

1 tbsp minced ginger

½ tsp ground black pepper

METHOD

1 Stir the ingredients for the sauce together and combine with the chicken. Oil a deep frypan or paella pan with the sesame oil and place the cabbage, onion, carrot, chilli, sweet potato, rice cakes and sesame leaves in the pan. Top with the chicken and any remaining sauce.

2 Place the pan over high heat and cook, covered, for 15 minutes. Stir the contents of the pan, and continue to cook, uncovered, for about a further 10 minutes, stirring occasionally until the chicken is cooked and the vegetables softened. Add a little water to the pan if it starts to get too dry. Serve straight from the pan.

NOTES

In Korea, *dak galbi* is made in a specific pan used just for this dish. It's very similar to a paella pan, and if you have one, it's a great substitute. If you have a double-handled frypan, that is fine too. Using a lid cooks things faster.

Serve this dish with a few *banchan* dishes (pages 128-129) and snack on them over a few drinks while waiting for the *dak galbi* to cook. Cooking at the table is supposed to be a leisurely event, so there's no rush to get the food cooked and eaten.

The perfect way to finish a meal of *dak galbi* is with some cooked rice. When the chicken is finished and there is a rich sauce left in the base of the pan, add rice and form into a thin pancake. You can even add some grated cheese. Fry until crisp and cut into squares to eat.

CHICKEN, COCONUT AND GALANGAL SOUP
Tom kha gai

SERVES 4 PREPARATION TIME 15 MINS **COOKING TIME 20 MINS**

Despite its reputation for being spicy, Thai cuisine is more about fragrance than heat. In this classic Thai soup the aromas of lemongrass, galangal, coriander and lime leaves flavour a light but creamy coconut broth.

INGREDIENTS

1 stalk lemongrass, woody end trimmed

5cm galangal, sliced

3 red bird's-eye chillies

2 coriander roots, roots and stalks separated, leaves picked and reserved to serve

1 litre Chicken Stock (page 33)

2 tbsp fish sauce, plus extra to serve

½ tsp salt

1 tbsp chopped palm sugar

4 kaffir lime leaves

2 cups button mushrooms, halved (or quartered if large)

400g chicken breast fillets, thinly sliced

200ml coconut cream

About 40ml lime juice

METHOD

1 With the flat of a knife or a heavy pestle, bruise the lemongrass, galangal, chillies and coriander roots and stems then add them to a large saucepan with the Chicken Stock, fish sauce, salt, palm sugar and lime leaves. Bring to a simmer and simmer, partially covered, for 10 minutes. Add the mushrooms and chicken and simmer for about 5 minutes, until the chicken is just cooked and the mushrooms have softened. Add the coconut cream and bring the pot back to a simmer. Adjust for seasoning with salt, fish sauce or additional sugar and remove from the heat.

2 Place 2 teaspoons of lime juice and a dash of fish sauce in the base of each serving bowl and ladle in about 1½ cups of hot soup. Scatter with coriander leaves and serve immediately.

NOTES

The success of this soup requires the flavour of the fragrant ingredients - lemongrass, galangal, chilli and kaffir lime - to infuse into the stock and for the stock to be balanced. Use fish sauce (savoury), sugar (sweet) and lime juice (sour) to produce a pleasant savoury flavour with just a hint of sweetness and sourness. Straw mushrooms are usually used in this dish and can be found in cans in Asian supermarkets, but I prefer to use fresh button mushrooms.

This is a great Thai dish for people who don't like spicy food. You can leave the chillies out and still create a fantastic, authentic flavour.

INDONESIAN GRILLED CHICKEN
Ayam bakar

SERVES 6 PREPARATION TIME 30 MINS **COOKING TIME 1 HOUR**

Grilled chicken is one of the most popular Indonesian dishes, either on its own or served as part of the popular mixed rice dish *nasi campur*. In this recipe, chicken Marylands are first simmered in a flavourful coconut gravy, then basted with sweet soy sauce and barbecued until crisped and irresistible.

INGREDIENTS

5 eschalots, peeled, or 1 large brown onion, peeled

3 bird's-eye chillies, or to taste

3 cloves garlic, peeled

3cm ginger, peeled and sliced

1 stalk lemongrass

¼ cup peanut oil, plus extra 2 tbsp for grilling

1 tbsp ground coriander

1 tsp turmeric powder

2 tsp salt

2 tbsp sugar

2 kaffir lime leaves, sliced

400ml coconut milk

6 chicken Marylands

½ cup *kecap manis*, plus extra, to serve

Cooked rice, to serve

Sliced cucumber and tomato, to serve

Sambal Belacan (page 28), to serve

METHOD

1 Place the eschalots, chillies, garlic, ginger and lemongrass in a food processor and process to a paste. Heat ¼ cup oil in a large saucepan and fry the paste, stirring frequently for about 10 minutes or until it is fragrant and starting to brown. Add the coriander, turmeric, salt, sugar, lime leaves and coconut milk and stir well. Add the chicken and bring to a simmer. Simmer, covered, for 30 minutes, turning occasionally until the chicken is cooked through and tender. Allow the chicken to cool in the remaining liquid then drain and set aside until ready to eat.

2 Heat a barbecue grill to low-medium. Mix the *kecap manis* with the 2 tbsp oil (or use the coconut oil separated from the stewing) and brush all over the chicken pieces. Grill the chicken until it is well browned and charred in places. Serve with rice, sliced cucumber, tomato, some Sambal Belacan and a little extra *kecap manis*.

NOTES

While you could serve this with cooked vegetables, the freshness of raw cucumber and tomato is a great balance to the hot sweet and savoury chicken.

The *kecap manis* acts as a sweet glaze that caramelises on the skin of the chicken on the grill. Because of the sugar in the glaze, it will blacken quickly, so be sure to use a low heat.

This is one of my go-to dishes when I'm having a barbecue. I stew a big pot of chicken the night before, then finish it on the grill when guests arrive.

LESSON 9
MEAT

Cooking with meat is not difficult, but it does require a little bit of knowledge to achieve the best results. In the previous lesson we learned about choosing cuts, resting and cooking on the bone as they relate to poultry. All those ideas apply equally importantly to meat. Whether it's pork, lamb or beef, choose your cuts carefully and specifically for the purpose you will use them for.

Where meat was once a delicacy in Asian cuisines, it is now common to eat it every day and at every meal. Meat is relatively cheap, but we seem to demand it cheaper and want more of it. I think that is the wrong approach. Meat is one food where quality over quantity is a great mantra. Good quality meat is fantastic and you don't need to eat a lot of it to feel full or appreciate it.

My tip is to buy the best quality meat you can afford. It might be slightly more expensive but more than almost any other type of food, meat is where you'll really taste the difference and experience the benefit of sourcing it from well-raised and ethically treated animals.

PREFERRED CUTS OF MEAT FOR ASIAN COOKERY

When it comes to cuts of meat, Asian cookery is not as prescriptive as Western cooking. Because the meat is often sliced thinly and cooked quickly, cuts which might be considered too tough for frying in Western cooking can be used with great results in wok-fried dishes.

I generally favour cuts that have a little fat on them, regardless of the style of cooking. Lean cuts of meat like tenderloin and fillet are a little too dry and flavourless for use in Asian food, but they can certainly also be used if you prefer them.

Pork

Pork belly is a very versatile cut for any style of cooking. It can be stewed or roasted in blocks, or thinly sliced for wok-fried dishes. Belly is also the preferred cut of pork for a lot of Japanese and Korean cooking where it is often grilled, fried or boiled. Other good cuts for Asian cooking include pork neck and leg, which have great flavour as well as enough fat to keep them moist. For wok-frying, thinly sliced pork leg or shoulder are also suitable.

Beef

While Chinese restaurants in the past in Australia boasted of using fillet steak, I've never considered it a great choice for wok-fried dishes. For wok-fried dishes you want a flavourful cut with just a little fat, and fillet steak is relatively mild in flavour. I usually use rump steak or sirloin that I thinly slice diagonally to the grain (see page 52), but topside and round are also good choices. For long braised dishes, chuck steak is perfect. In Korea, beef rib (or *kalbi*) is one of the favourite cuts for grilling. Traditionally the meat is carefully unrolled from the bone, keeping the bone at one end. More recently the Korean community in Los Angeles developed the LA kalbi, where a whole rack of ribs is thinly cut into strips through the bone for easy grilling.

Lamb and mutton

Lamb and mutton are less common in East Asia, but are popular meats in Islamic Asian countries like Malaysia and Indonesia. In Japan, lamb is actually viewed as a healthy alternative to beef, which sounds strange until you see the fatty marbling of Japanese wagyu. For wok-fried lamb dishes, I tend to use lamb leg, chump, shoulder or rump sliced thinly across the grain.

MARINADES

Marinades can be useful for adding flavour to meat and poultry, but to marinade effectively you need to know a bit about how they work. Marinades only penetrate a few millimetres into meats, and as such most of their effect occurs at the surface. Marinating will be more effective on meat that is sliced thinly to give it a greater surface area in contact with the marinade.

Like sauces added during cooking, Asian marinades serve mainly for seasoning, but can also include flavours like garlic and ginger, and around Southeast Asia, herbs and spices too. An Asian marinade generally contains three key kinds of ingredients. Each plays an important role:

1 **Saltiness and/or Umami:**
   An Asian marinade acts a little like a brine, keeping meat moist as it cooks and using salty ingredients (such as soy sauce, fish sauce, or salt itself) to season the meat and help the marinade to penetrate the surface. Umami flavours are enhanced by heat (particularly by browning Maillard reactions) and so they also make great additions to marinades.

2 **Sweetness and/or Starch**
   Because the main effect of marinades is at the surface of the meat, a sweet or starchy component is very important. As the marinade cooks on the surface, the sugar from the sweet ingredients caramelises and helps stick the marinade to the meat. Starch has a similar effect, thickening the marinade and holding more of its flavour to the meat.

3 **Oil and/or Alcohol**
   Adding oil or alcohol to a marinade helps to develop the flavour of the marinade itself, particularly where it contains herbs or spices. Flavourful molecules soluble in oil and alcohol can more easily transfer their flavour throughout the marinade when it contains one or both of these ingredients.

Another major point of difference between Asia and Western marinades is that Asian marinades rarely include acidic ingredients. Acidity in a Western marinade is added to tenderise larger cuts of meat. Asian marinades are used most often on meat that has been sliced, and acidic ingredients in marinades can leave sliced meat with a mushy texture.

Marinating time is also less important. When marinating meats to season them for stir-frying, even just a few minutes is fine. Sweet or starchy ingredients in the marinade will hold the seasoning to the outside of the meat regardless of how long it marinates for. As the marinade contains no acid, however, the meat can be left marinating for longer periods, and even stored or frozen in the marinade.

For marinades that are strongly flavoured, such as for Beef Satay (page 189), a longer marinating time will allow more of the flavour of the marinade to develop and penetrate the meat.

A marinade is more effective at room temperature than it is in the fridge. You can leave a marinating meat covered at room temperature for up to 2 hours if you plan to refrigerate it again before cooking, or up to 4 hours if you plan to cook it without further refrigeration.

BEEF SATAY
Satay daging

MASS ABOUT 50 SKEWERS PREPARATION TIME 1 HOUR + OVERNIGHT MARINATING **COOKING TIME 40 MINS**

Satay are found all over Southeast Asia, and although I might be biased because I was born there, I think Malaysian satay are the best. This is my Aunty Ivy's recipe, and it's fantastic. You could easily substitute chicken for the beef if you prefer.

INGREDIENTS

1kg beef topside

50 bamboo skewers, soaked in water

½ cup peanut oil, for brushing

Cucumber and red onion pieces, to serve

Marinade

1 medium brown onion, peeled and roughly chopped

2 tbsp ground coriander

1 tbsp ground cumin

1 tsp ground fennel

1 tsp turmeric powder

3 stalks lemongrass, tender inner core only, finely sliced

4 tbsp sugar

2 tbsp dark soy sauce

4 tbsp peanut oil

Peanut sauce

10 large dried chillies, deseeded and soaked in hot water for 20 minutes

2 medium brown onions, peeled and sliced

4 cloves garlic, peeled

2 stalks lemongrass, tender inner core only, finely sliced

1 tbsp *belacan* (shrimp paste)

1 tsp ground coriander

1 tsp ground cumin

1 tbsp tamarind paste, loosened in ¼ cup hot water

¼ cup peanut oil

300g ground roasted peanuts

400ml coconut cream

2 tbsp sugar

1 tsp salt

METHOD

1 Chill or freeze the beef for 1 hour to firm the meat then slice it thinly against the grain. Slice into 5cm pieces.

2 For the beef marinade, combine all the ingredients in a blender or food processor and purée. Combine the beef with the marinade ingredients and refrigerate overnight.

3 Soak the bamboo skewers in cold water for at least 1 hour and thread the beef onto the skewers. Thread each piece onto the skewer two or three times to hold it in place, and finish each skewer with a squeeze to press the beef close to the skewer.

4 For the peanut sauce, combine the chillies, onions, garlic, lemongrass, *belacan*, coriander and cumin in a blender and blend to a purée. Mix the tamarind pulp with the ¼ cup hot water, rubbing through with your fingers or a spoon to loosen the seeds from the pulp, pass through a sieve and discard the seeds, reserving the thick tamarind water.

5 Heat the oil in a medium saucepan over medium heat and fry the blended paste for about 10-15 minutes, stirring occasionally until very fragrant. Add the peanuts and coconut cream and bring to a simmer. Add the tamarind water, sugar and salt and simmer for a further 5-10 minutes, until the sauce starts to form an oily gloss on the surface.

6 Grill the satays on a hot barbecue, grill pan or frypan, basting regularly with extra oil and turning regularly for about 5 minutes until cooked through. If using a barbecue, grill the satay on the hotplate side rather than the open grill side, or if cooking under an overhead grill, cover the bamboo part of the skewers with a piece of aluminium foil to help stop the skewers from burning under direct heat.

NOTES

With satay the flavour of the skewered meat is more important than the peanut sauce. A good satay should taste great even without any sauce.

Keep the tops of the lemongrass and tie them together at the thin end. Bash the thick ends and use them as a brush to baste the satay with oil when cooking.

Slicing the meat thinly and skewering each piece multiple times helps the meat stay on the skewer and stops it from spinning during cooking.

DONGPO PORK

SERVES 4 PREPARATION TIME 15 MINS **COOKING TIME 3 HOURS**

Red-cooking is one of the simplest cooking methods in Chinese cuisine. The name comes from the glossy deep red-brown colour produced from the slow braising of meat in soy sauce and sugar. This technique has influenced dishes all over the region, from Japan's *buta kakuni* and Okinawan *rafute* to Thailand's *khao ka moo*. One of the most famous versions of red-cooking is Hangzhou's *dongpo* pork, slow simmered until the pork is nearly falling apart and the sauce is reduced to a thick gloss. It's sweet, savoury and sticky, with just a hint of fragrant tea.

INGREDIENTS

1kg pork belly, bones removed

1 tbsp peanut oil

2 tbsp soy sauce

½ cup dark soy sauce

½ cup Shaoxing wine

4 tbsp yellow rock sugar or caster sugar

1 tbsp Chinese tea leaves, brewed
   into 1 cup of hot water and strained
   (optional)

5cm ginger, peeled, sliced and bruised

4 thick spring onions, trimmed and cut
   into 5cm lengths

Cooked rice or steamed Chinese buns,
   to serve

METHOD

1 Place the pork in a large pot of cold water and bring to a simmer. Simmer for 10 minutes, then remove, drain and discard the water. Rest the pork for 10 minutes, then slice into 7cm × 5cm blocks. The pork will not be cooked through.

2 Heat the peanut oil in a wok or large frypan. Brown the pork pieces in batches on all sides and set aside.

3 In a claypot or medium saucepan, bring the soy sauces, wine, sugar and brewed tea to the boil and add the ginger and spring onions. Add the pork skin-side down and top up with more water until the pork is just covered. Bring to a simmer and simmer, covered, for 2–3 hours until the pork is very tender.

4 Gently remove the pork from the liquid, place in a serving dish and set aside. Bring the liquid to the boil and reduce to a thick glaze. Pour the glaze over the pork and serve immediately with rice or steamed Chinese buns.

NOTES

The goal of the dish is a combination of textures: layers of tender pork, silky fat and delicate skin all tied together with a luxurious, sticky sauce glossed by the fat rendered from the pork.

For a variation, try adding a few star anise to the pot when simmering. A reaction between aromatic compounds in star anise and sulphur compounds in onion actually creates meaty, umami flavours.

Yellow rock sugar is available from Asian grocery stores. It's often used in savoury Chinese dishes but ordinary caster sugar is a good substitute.

LAMB WITH GINGER AND SPRING ONION

SERVES 2-4 PREPARATION TIME 10 MINS + 30 MINS MARINATING **COOKING TIME 10 MINS**

In the same way that ginger in many Asian dishes is used to moderate fishy aromas in seafood, it is used here to tackle the stronger, meaty flavour of lamb.

INGREDIENTS

500g lamb leg, thinly sliced

2 tbsp vegetable oil

2cm ginger, peeled and finely shredded

4 thick spring onions, cut into 7cm
   lengths and thinly sliced lengthways

2 cloves garlic, peeled and minced

Meat marinade

2 tbsp dark soy sauce

1 tbsp Shaoxing wine

2 tsp sesame oil

½ tsp sugar

1 tbsp cornflour

Sauce

2 tbsp stock or water

1 tbsp dark soy sauce

1 tbsp Shaoxing wine

½ tsp cornflour

1 tsp sugar

METHOD

1 Combine the marinade ingredients, add the meat and set aside for at least 30 minutes, but preferably overnight.

2 Add half the oil to a hot wok and fry the meat in batches until well browned. Set aside. Brush out the wok, add the rest of the oil and fry the ginger and spring onions until fragrant, then add the garlic and fry for a further 30 seconds. Return the meat to the wok and toss.

3 Combine the sauce ingredients. Make a well in the centre of the ingredients in the wok, pour the sauce into the well and bring to the boil, tossing the meat through the sauce for a minute or so until it thickens and coats the meat.

NOTES

Don't be tempted to 'bulk-up' this dish by adding other vegetables. If you want to add other vegetables to the meal, just make a separate dish.

It's very important to keep the sauce separate until the end - adding it too early will stop the meat from browning.

Lamb (or more usually mutton) is a popular meat in Chinese cooking in the far northern and western regions. You could also use chicken or beef for this dish.

BISTEK

SERVES 6 PREPARATION TIME 15 MINS + 1 HOUR MARINATING COOKING TIME 15 MINS

The sour and savoury flavours of this easy Filipino dish really are characteristic of the cuisine. Along with *sinigang* (page 41), many Filipinos consider a plate of *bistek* the true taste of home.

INGREDIENTS

800g rump steak

½ cup dark soy sauce

Juice of 2 lemons, plus lemon wedges
   to serve

1 tsp sugar

6 cloves garlic, peeled and minced

¼ cup vegetable oil

2 red onions, peeled and cut into
   1cm rings

Ground black pepper, to serve

Patismansi (page 28), to serve
   (optional)

METHOD

1   Slice the rump steak on a steep diagonal to produce large pieces of steak around 1cm thick. Combine the steak with the soy sauce, lemon juice, sugar and garlic and marinate for at least 1 hour.

2   Heat a little of the oil in a large frypan over low-medium heat and fry the onion rings until caramelised and softened. Remove the onions from the pan and set aside.

3   Add the remaining oil to the pan and increase the heat to high. Remove the beef from the marinade and fry in batches until well browned on both sides then transfer to a warmed serving plate. Add the marinade to the pan and simmer for 5-10 minutes until the sauce is reduced and slightly thickened. Place the onion on top of the cooked beef and pour over a little of the reduced marinade. Serve with extra lemon wedges, ground black pepper and perhaps a little Patismansi if you like.

NOTES

You can substitute a stewing cut of beef such as chuck. Instead of removing the sliced beef from the pan after browning, just add the marinade in with the beef with a cup of water, and simmer for about an hour until the beef is tender.

Instead of sliced rump, a simpler option would be to use thin, pre-cut minute steaks.

STEAMED SPARE RIBS WITH BLACK BEANS

SERVES 6 PREPARATION TIME 15 MINS + 15 MINS MARINATING **COOKING TIME 25 MINS**

This is one dish that I just can't let pass by on the *yum cha* trolley, but it also makes a great meal in itself. Use skinless pork belly if it's your first time trying this dish, as it's a little easier to cut and cook.

INGREDIENTS

800g pork spare ribs, or 750g skinless pork belly

2 tbsp salted black beans

2 tbsp Shaoxing wine

1 tsp grated ginger

2 cloves garlic, peeled and grated

3 tbsp cornflour

1 tsp sugar

1 bird's-eye chilli, sliced

¼ tsp white pepper

½ tsp salt

METHOD

1 Cut the spare ribs into 4cm lengths, or belly into 4cm cubes.

2 In a mortar or strong bowl, mix together the remaining ingredients and very lightly crush the black beans with a pestle or spoon. Mix the marinade through the pork and set aside to marinate for at least 15 minutes.

3 Arrange the pork in a single layer over a heatproof serving plate that will fit inside your bamboo steamer. Bring the water under the steamer to a boil and place the plate of pork inside. Cover the steamer and steam for 15-20 minutes until the pork is cooked through. Remove the plate from the steamer and allow to stand for a minute before serving.

NOTES

Yum cha (also called *dim sum* in some countries) is the Cantonese version of brunch. Eaten in the late morning, the meal consists of a selection of dumplings and other small dishes (often chosen from trolleys pushed around the restaurant from table to table), all washed down with pots of hot tea.

Salted black beans are a strong source of umami. Rather than buying bottled black bean sauce for cooking, try pounding a few black beans in a mortar and pestle with some Shaoxing wine and sugar instead. It's cheaper, tastier and really very easy.

The 'piggy' smell from some pork can be quite unpleasant and often puts people off eating it. It's known as 'boar taint' and is caused by hormones in male pigs that have not been castrated. Asian butchers will often sell pork from female pigs separately, so that customers know it will be free from boar taint.

THAI GRILLED PORK
Muu yang

SERVES 4-6 PREPARATION TIME 10 MINS + 1 HOUR MARINATING **COOKING TIME 10 MINS**

It's hard to decide what's more important to the flavour of this dish - the sweet and savoury marinade or the spicy, textured *nam jim jaew* dipping sauce. They both work together perfectly for one of the tastiest Thai dishes I know.

INGREDIENTS

750g pork neck, sliced into 1cm slices

Nam Jim Jaew, to serve (page 29)

Sliced cucumber, to serve

Marinade

2 tbsp fish sauce

1 tbsp soy sauce

2 tbsp caster sugar

½ tsp salt

3 cloves garlic, peeled and minced

¼ tsp black pepper

¼ cup coconut milk or 2 tbsp vegetable oil

METHOD

1   Combine the pork and the marinade ingredients in a bowl or press-seal bag and marinate for at least 1 hour, but preferably overnight.

2   Grill the pork slices on a barbecue or hot grill pan for about 3 minutes each side, or until cooked through. Rest for a further 3 minutes, then slice into strips on an angle. Serve with the Nam Jim Jaew and slices of cucumber.

NOTES

Pork neck is a delicious and affordable cut. It has thick bolts of fat running through the meat that keep it moist when grilled, fried or roasted. It is sometimes sold in Australia labelled as 'pork scotch fillet', as its round shape and 'eye' of fat can resemble the much more expensive beef cut.

BRAISED MINCED PORK
Lu rou fan

SERVES 4 PREPARATION TIME 15 MINS **COOKING TIME 1 HOUR**

Chinese and Japanese influences are obvious in this popular Taiwanese comfort food.
The braised pork is loaded with Chinese flavours, but the balance provided by the sweet
and sour pickled mustard greens is a combination reminiscent of a Japanese *donburi*.

INGREDIENTS

2 tbsp peanut oil

500g pork belly, skin-off, coarsely
  chopped, or 500g pork mince

4 cloves garlic, peeled and minced

½ cup fried eschalots

½ tsp salt

1 tbsp caster sugar

1 tsp Chinese five spice powder

1 star anise

2 tbsp soy sauce

2 tbsp dark soy sauce

2 tbsp Shaoxing wine

2 cups Coarse Stock (page 32), Chicken
  Stock (page 33) or water

1 tbsp cornflour mixed with 2 tbsp cold
  water

4 hard-boiled eggs, peeled

6 cups cooked rice, warm to serve

2 thin spring onions, finely chopped

Pickled mustard greens or Oiled Greens
  (page 133), to serve

METHOD

1 Heat the peanut oil in a medium saucepan over high
heat and fry the pork belly until well browned. Add the
garlic and fried eschalots and mix well, then add the
salt, sugar, five spice powder and star anise and fry until
fragrant. Add the soy sauces, Shaoxing wine and stock
and bring to a simmer. Simmer, covered, for 40 minutes,
stirring occasionally.

2 Stir in the cornflour mixture and cook for a further
minute, or until the sauce is quite thick and silky. Add the
hard-boiled eggs and stand until ready to serve.

3 To serve, place spoonfuls of the minced pork and an egg
over rice and scatter with spring onions. Serve with the
pickled mustard greens or Oiled Greens.

NOTES

Rather than warming hard-boiled eggs in the braising liquid, you could leave
them out and serve this with tea eggs instead. They're eggs that have been
boiled, cracked and steeped in a liquid made from soy sauce and tea, giving a
marbled appearance.

Braising the crispy fried eschalots in this dish is a very Taiwanese technique,
and it adds an interesting texture to the mince.

PORK CHOP RICE
Pai gu fan

SERVES 4 PREPARATION TIME 10 MINS + 1 HOUR MARINATING **COOKING TIME 20 MINS**

This has to be one of the most famous dishes to come out of Taiwan, and it's their answer to Japanese *tonkatsu* or German schnitzel. A thinly beaten pork chop is fried in crispy sweet potato flour and served with rice flavoured with minced pork, egg and vegetables.

INGREDIENTS

4 pork chops, bone-in

3 cloves garlic, peeled and minced

2 tbsp soy sauce

2 tbsp Shaoxing wine

1 tbsp caster sugar

1 tsp Chinese five spice powder

¼ tsp white pepper

About 500ml vegetable oil, for frying

1 cup sweet potato flour or cornflour

6 cups cooked rice, warm to serve

¾ cup Braised Minced Pork (page 202),
   to serve (optional)

Pickled mustard greens, or Oiled Greens
   (page 133), to serve (optional)

METHOD

1   Score the surface of the chops on one side with light cuts 2cm apart. Lightly pound them until they are 1cm thick, then place in a press-seal bag and add the garlic, soy sauce, Shaoxing wine, sugar, five spice powder and pepper and massage well. Seal the bag and marinate for at least 1 hour.

2   Fill a large frypan or wok with vegetable oil to a depth of about 1cm and heat to 165°C. Dredge the pork chops in the flour, then shallow-fry in two batches for about 6 minutes, turning halfway through cooking. Drain well and rest for 5 minutes. Serve the pork chop sliced, with rice topped with a little Braised Minced Pork, pickled mustard greens or Oiled Greens.

NOTES

Another common accompaniment to this dish in Taiwan is the Japanese sweet, yellow daikon pickle known as *takuan*.

This is a great dish for extending a meal of Taiwanese Braised Minced Pork (page 202). Just add enough of the pork and its sauce to moisten and flavour the rice, and serve it along with the pork chop.

If you prefer your pork chop crispier rather than juicier, beat it until it is only half a centimetre thin. It will have a larger surface area to hold more of the coating.

GLAZED PORK DONBURI
Teriyaki butadon

SERVES 4   PREPARATION TIME 15 MINS   **COOKING TIME 15 MINS**

For me there's not much better than an easy *donburi* dinner. This pork version
is one of my favourite quick weeknight comfort foods.

INGREDIENTS

2 tsp vegetable oil

600g pork belly, skin and bone
   removed, sliced into ½cm slices then
   again into 10cm pieces

¾ cup Teriyaki Glaze (page 148)

6 cups cooked short-grain rice, warm

1 sheet nori, quartered, to serve

2 cups very finely shredded cabbage,
   to serve

4 hard-boiled eggs, to serve

2 thin spring onions, trimmed and finely
   sliced

Shichimi togarashi, to serve (optional)

METHOD

1   Heat a very large frypan over high heat and add the
oil. Fry the pork belly until browned on both sides and add
½ cup of the teriyaki glaze. Bring the glaze to the boil and
turn the pork through the glaze until it thickens and coats
the pork. Remove the pork from the pan and rest for a few
minutes. Add the remaining glaze to the pan, stir to pick up
any caramelised bits at the bottom of the pan and simmer
the glaze until it thickens.

2   Divide the rice among four deep bowls and spoon or
brush over the thick glaze remaining in the pan. Top with
a square of nori, ½ cup of shredded cabbage and arrange
the pork slices on top. Add a halved hard-boiled egg,
scatter with spring onions and sprinkle with a little *shichimi
togarashi* (if using).

NOTES

Shichimi togarashi is a Japanese mix of seven spices. The components can
vary but it may include chilli, dried lemon or orange, nori, white and black
sesame seeds, and hemp or rape seeds. It's available from most Asian
grocers.

Japanese cuisine uses a lot of shredded cabbage to lighten and balance
meaty dishes. Use a mandoline to shred it really finely. If you don't have a
mandoline you can just shred it finely with a sharp knife. My friend Jun once
told me his father uses a cheese slicer for the same purpose.

Try this with chicken or pork mince instead for an easy dinner.

LESSON 10
SWEETS

SWEETS AND DESSERTS IN ASIAN CUISINES

Whether at home or at a restaurant, a casual meal in Asia often ends with a simple plate of fruits rather than a specially prepared dessert. The fruit cleans the palate without leaving you feeling too heavy.

Sweet foods in Asian cuisines are usually eaten as snacks over tea or coffee between regular mealtimes. There are exceptions, however, and Cantonese cuisine often has simple desserts served at the end of a banquet meal such as Sweet Red Bean Soup (page 216). Small sweets similar to petit-fours are also common at the end of a Japanese formal *kaiseki* meal.

Desserts are becoming more popular in Asian cuisines, but they are still quite simple. A scoop of Green Tea Ice Cream (page 212) is a fantastic end to a Japanese meal, and Coconut Sticky Rice with Mango (page 224) is gaining popularity in Thai food as a dessert dish rather than as a snack.

Even though desserts at the end of meals is relatively less common around Asia, Asian cuisines have an incredibly rich and varied range of sweets. Japan has its *wagashi*, sweets based on bean pastes, sugars and jellies. Malaysia has an extraordinary variety of *kuih*, small bites made from glutinous rice, coconut milk, palm sugar, pandan leaves or other common ingredients. One of my favourite *kuih* made from palm sugar and coconut milk is on page 223. China too has a long list of sweet foods encompassing everything from traditional sweet soups like Glutinous Rice Balls in Ginger Syrup (page 219) to small tarts and jellies served at *yum cha*.

It is sometimes said that Asian sweets are less sweet than their Western counterparts, but I have never found that to be the case. Perhaps that reputation has come about from the tendency of Asian sweets to include ingredients that Western cuisines might more readily associate with savoury foods. Beans are commonly used in Asian sweets whether in Red Bean Paste (page 215) or simply whole in some Southeast Asian dishes. One of my favourite childhood desserts in Malaysia, *ice kacang*, often contains creamed corn and noodles made from mung bean flour. But regardless of the ingredients used, there is a fundamentally different approach to seasoning Asian sweets than Western ones.

SEASONING DESSERTS

The most important difference between Asian sweets and Western sweets is in what is left out. In Western cooking, the opposite of sweet flavour is considered to be savoury, and as such we tend to think of sweets as having an absence of salty or savoury flavours. (In truth, however, salty and umami undertones are quite common in Western sweets, from pie crusts to caramel.)

In Asian cuisine, the opposite of sweetness is sourness, and so rather than withholding savoury flavour from sweet dishes, it is sourness that is rarely found in Asian sweets.

Adding saltiness, umami and even bitterness to sweet foods is common in Asian cuisines, and many popular ingredients for sweets are used for these properties. Some of these are discussed on the opposite page.

Seasoning enhances the overall taste of the dish, drawing out the natural flavours of ingredients just as it does in savoury dishes, and the presence of salt actually promotes the effect of sweetness on your taste buds. Sweet foods eaten with a little salt actually taste sweeter.

As a child I remember my grandmother sprinkling salt on pineapple and other fruits when one was found to be a little sour. With each mouthful there would be an initial hit of saltiness that would soon give way to deliciously sweet pineapple. I thought it was magical at the time, and now that I know it is just the science of our taste buds at work, it is magical still. The same effect is used in Thai cuisine where sour green mango is eaten as a snack dipped in salt and chilli powder.

Pandan (fresh) - Pandan leaves are a fragrant addition to both sweet and savoury dishes. Slightly similar to vanilla, pandan has a toasty flavour that is reminiscent of the aromas produced by Maillard reactions. **1**

Coconut cream **2a** and coconut milk **2b** are both extracted from a fresh coconut in the same way. In most Southeast Asian cuisines they are not treated as different ingredients, and are just referred to as 'thick' and 'thin' coconut milk. The flesh of the coconut is grated and pressed, sometimes with added water, to extract the fat and juice. What we call 'coconut cream' is the thicker pressing, with a higher proportion of oil and solids than 'coconut milk', which is thinner.

Green tea powder (also known as *matcha*) is a very finely ground powder from tea leaves that have been specially produced to enhance their colour and umami flavour, and its flavour and colour is quite different to ordinary leaf tea. Because of its bitter and umami characteristics, it's used in Japanese cuisine in both sweet and savoury dishes. **3**

Red beans (*adzuki*) are probably the most common sweet ingredient across Asia. They're made into pastes, used as fillings for sweet dumplings and buns and are found in soups and sweet drinks all over Asia. **4**

Agar agar (also known as *kanten*) is a natural extract of algae that has been used in Asian cuisines for centuries. It is often used to set liquids into firm jellies for sweets. It's available as long transparent strands or ground into fine powder. **5**

Glutinous rice flour - The ground flour from glutinous rice is used in many sweet foods from Japanese *mochi* to sweet soup dumplings in Chinese cuisine. It contains no gluten and is very easy to handle. **6**

Black sesame seeds - Both black and white sesame seeds are used in many Asian sweets. They are ground to pastes with sugar and used as fillings for dumplings, baked with honey into crisp biscuits, and even made into ice cream. **7**

GREEN TEA ICE CREAM
Matcha aisu

MAKES ABOUT 1 LITRE PREPARATION TIME 5 MINS **COOKING TIME 10 MINS + 5 HOURS CHILLING**

Although green tea ice cream is now found all over Japan and in Japanese restaurants abroad, it only really became popular in the 1990s. It's simple to make at home.

INGREDIENTS

400ml full-cream milk

300ml pouring cream

6 egg yolks

½ cup caster sugar

20g green tea powder (*matcha*)

METHOD

1 Combine the milk and cream in a small saucepan and bring to a simmer, then remove from the heat.

2 Beat the egg yolks and caster sugar until pale and combined, then beat in the green tea powder. Slowly whisk the hot milk mixture into the egg mixture, then strain everything back into the saucepan and stir over medium heat until the mixture coats the back of a spoon.

3 Transfer to a bowl and cool first to room temperature, then in the fridge for about an hour until chilled.

4 Churn in an ice cream machine according to the manufacturer's instructions, then set in the freezer for at least 2 hours.

NOTES

You can make ice cream without an ice cream machine – just place the mixture in the freezer and whisk it vigorously every 30 minutes until it sets too firmly to whisk. It will take about 4 hours to freeze.

Green tea powder is available from the Japanese section of Asian grocery stores. Don't try to substitute ordinary leaf green tea.

RED BEAN PASTE
Anko

MAKES 2 CUPS PREPARATION TIME 5 MINS + OVERNIGHT SOAKING **COOKING TIME 1½ HRS**

Red bean paste is the basis for many delicious Asian sweets in China, Japan and throughout Southeast Asia. The smooth variety known in Japanese as *koshian* is the most popular, but the chunky variety, *tsubuan*, is a little easier to make. It's up to you which variety you want to make, as they both follow the same method.

INGREDIENTS

1 cup dried red beans (*adzuki*)

1 cup caster sugar

A pinch salt

METHOD

1   Soak the beans in cold water overnight and rinse well. Cover the beans with plenty of fresh cold water and bring to the boil. Discard the water and add new cold water just to the top of the beans and simmer, covered, for 1 hour, or until the beans can be easily crushed. If necessary, add additional hot water regularly to keep the beans under the surface.

2   Stir half the sugar into the beans and boil, uncovered, for 1 minute, then add the remaining sugar and a pinch of salt, stir and continue to boil until the water evaporates and the bean mixture reaches the consistency of thick, lumpy honey. This will take about 20 minutes. Transfer to a tray to cool. The paste will thicken as it cools. This is *tsubuan*.

3   If you prefer a smooth paste (*koshian*), grind the cooled paste with a mortar and pestle and pass it through a sieve to remove any pieces of skin.

NOTES

Red bean paste is used in other desserts such as Anmitsu (page 220), or Sesame Balls (page 227). In Nagoya in central Japan it's even eaten on buttered toast with whipped cream.

The paste can be refrigerated or frozen - just wrap with plastic wrap in individual portions and keep in the fridge for up to a month, or freeze it for up to six months.

SWEET RED BEAN SOUP

SERVES 6 PREPARATION TIME 10 MINS **COOKING TIME 2 HOURS**

Sweet red bean soup is ubiquitous across Asia, popping up in hundreds of different ways in many and varied dishes. There are thin versions served chilled with coconut milk in Vietnam; thick ones served warm with grilled rice cakes in Japan; versions with sago in Malaysia; and even savoury porridge-type varieties in Korea. Whatever your preference, they all start the same way – with a simple pot of boiled beans.

INGREDIENTS

1 cup red beans (*adzuki*)

2 litres water

¾ cup sugar

¼ tsp salt

1 litre vanilla ice cream, to serve
  (optional)

NOTES

Other variations exist around Asia, including with sago or coconut cream. Korean cuisine also includes a savoury red bean porridge (*patjuk*), in which the beans are cooked with rice.

The more you crush the beans, the more the soup will thicken. If you prefer a very thick soup, add less water or boil the beans uncovered for longer.

METHOD

1 Wash the red beans and place in a small saucepan. Cover with plenty of cold water and bring to the boil. Boil for 1 minute, then drain and discard the water. Return the beans to the pot, add 2 litres water, bring to a simmer, then simmer, covered, for 1½ hours until a thick soup forms, occasionally skimming any scum that rises to the surface. Stir in the sugar and salt and roughly crush the beans in the pot with a spoon or masher. Cook for a few minutes until the sugar is dissolved.

2 Serve the soup on its own either warm or chilled, or in one of the following styles:

With ice cream: Probably my favourite way to eat this soup is warm with a scoop of vanilla ice cream dropped in when serving. The warm soup and cold ice cream are a great contrast.

Dumplings: Make one serve of unfilled Glutinous Rice Dumplings (page 219) and add to the soup. The dumplings can be cooked directly in the soup.

Chinese: Serve chilled in summer and warm in winter. It can be flavoured with spices such as cinnamon, dates and dried tangerine peel.

Japanese: Serve with dumplings as above (*shiruko*), or with grilled glutinous rice cakes (*mochi*) in place of the dumplings (*zenzai*).

Okinawan: Serve cold over shaved ice with condensed milk and a few dumplings (*zenzai*).

Vietnamese: Serve a slightly thinner version chilled in a glass of ice topped with coconut milk (*che dau do*).

GLUTINOUS RICE DUMPLINGS IN GINGER SYRUP
Tang yuan

SERVES 6 PREPARATION TIME 1 HOUR **COOKING TIME 20 MINS**

This sweet is traditionally made and eaten as a family affair on the day of the lunar calendar's winter solstice (or midwinter) in late December, even in the Southern Hemisphere where the seasons are opposite. The pink and white balls in sweet syrup symbolise prosperity and togetherness.

INGREDIENTS

250g glutinous rice flour

1 tbsp potato flour

About 100ml water

100g palm sugar, roughly chopped

A few drops red food colouring (optional)

Syrup

1 cup sugar

1½ litres water

2cm ginger, sliced and bruised

2 pandan leaves (optional)

NOTES

The texture of this dough is very different from more common stretchy, kneaded doughs containing gluten that are used for pasta, noodles and baking. It is brittle and dry but still holds together.

Don't leave the dumplings in the syrup for too long – if the dish is going to stand for longer than 15 minutes it's best to remove the dumplings from the syrup and keep them covered in a bowl. You can then re-combine them and reheat to serve.

There are many regional varieties of this dish. To make the Malaysian classic *onde-onde*, purée 4 pandan leaves with the water and strain to produce a bright-green liquid to add to the dough and roll the cooked dumplings in shredded coconut.

METHOD

1   Make a dough by mixing the glutinous rice flour and potato flour together with just enough water to bring it together into a solid mass. Knead the dough until smooth. If using food colouring, divide the dough into two equal parts and knead in enough red food colouring to tint one part of the dough light pink. Rest the dough for 15 minutes.

2   Pinch off teaspoon-sized pieces of dough and flatten them with your hands. Place a piece of chopped palm sugar in the centre and roll the dough between your palms to make balls about 1½cm in diameter.

3   For the syrup, bring all the ingredients except the pandan leaves to the boil in a large pot and simmer for 10 minutes. Add the pandan leaves, if using, and simmer for a further 5 minutes.

4   Bring a separate pot of water to a rolling boil and add the dumplings in batches, tossing them through the water for just 20 seconds to rinse off some of the loose starch (this will keep the syrup clear), then transfer the dumplings to the simmering syrup.

5   Simmer the dumplings until they rise to the surface of the syrup (about 2 minutes). Serve warm with plenty of the syrup.

ANMITSU

SERVES 4 PREPARATION TIME 15 MINS **COOKING TIME 10 MINS + 30 MINS SETTING**

In Japan, *anmitsu* is popular served with coffee for afternoon tea. It's a bit like a Japanese sundae - just fill a bowl with a few of your favourite things and you're good to go.

INGREDIENTS

2 cups mixed, chopped fruit (see below)

1 cup Red Bean Paste (page 215)

4 scoops Green Tea Ice Cream (page 212)

10 unfilled Glutinous Rice Dumplings (page 219)

Agar agar jelly

2 cups water

2 tsp agar agar powder, or 5g agar agar

2 tbsp caster sugar

Black sugar syrup (*kuromitsu*)

1 cup dark brown sugar or Japanese black sugar

2 tbsp caster sugar

1 cup water

METHOD

1   For the agar agar jelly, combine the water and agar agar in a small saucepan and bring to a simmer. Simmer, stirring regularly for about 5 minutes until the agar agar is completely dissolved. Add the sugar and continue to simmer for just a minute until the sugar is dissolved. Pour into a 20cm square cake tin and allow to cool to room temperature. Transfer to the fridge and chill for half an hour to set firm, then cut into 2cm cubes.

2   For the black sugar syrup, combine the sugars and water in a small saucepan, bring to a simmer and simmer for 5 minutes, or until the syrup thickens. Set aside to cool.

3   To assemble the dessert, place the agar agar cubes in the bottom of a bowl, arrange the fruits on top, add a scoop of Red Bean Paste and a scoop of Green Tea Ice Cream. Serve with the black sugar syrup on the side.

NOTES

Served without the red bean paste, this dessert is known as *mitsumame*.

Japanese black sugar (*kokutou*) is a hard and brittle unrefined sugar that's used to make *kuromitsu*, the black sugar syrup. You can find it in Japanese grocers, but dark brown sugar works well as a substitute.

Choose fruits that are in season. In summer, this is a great dessert with peaches, plums and other stone fruits.

COCONUT AND PALM SUGAR JELLIES
Agar agar gula melaka santan

MAKES ABOUT 25 PIECES PREPARATION TIME 10 MINS **COOKING TIME 10 MINS + 1 HOUR SETTING**

While it might look like it's set in two different layers, this clever dessert uses the natural properties of the coconut milk to striking visual effect. The oil in the coconut milk causes it to rise to the top as the jelly sets, creating distinct layers.

INGREDIENTS

600ml water, or 300ml water mixed with 300ml coconut water

2 pandan leaves, tied in a knot

150g palm sugar, roughly chopped

50g caster sugar

3 tsp agar agar powder or agar agar threads

400ml coconut milk

¼ tsp salt

METHOD

1   Combine water and coconut water, if using, pandan leaves, palm sugar, caster sugar and agar agar powder in a medium saucepan. Bring to a simmer and simmer, uncovered, for 5 minutes, or until the agar agar is completely dissolved.

2   Mix together the coconut milk and salt and stir well to remove any lumps. Add the coconut milk mixture to the saucepan and return to a simmer. Remove from the heat and pour into a 20cm square cake tin lined with plastic wrap. Allow to stand undisturbed until the mixture firms and reaches room temperature, then carefully move it to the fridge to chill for at least 1 hour.

3   Remove the set jelly from the tin and cut into diamonds to serve.

NOTES

If the layers in your jelly are not separating, it's probably due to the agar agar setting too quickly. Try reducing the amount of agar agar powder, as different brands will have different strengths.

Unlike gelatine, agar agar sets at room temperature - the jelly should be set before you move it to the fridge. While with gelatine a jelly should be soft and silky, the goal of a good agar agar jelly is a firm, almost crunchy, texture.

Try the same setting process with sweetened water with fruit in it, or even just with fruit juice.

COCONUT STICKY RICE WITH MANGO
Khao niaow ma muang

SERVES 6 PREPARATION TIME 10 MINS **COOKING TIME 20 MINS**

Sweet and slightly salty rice is matched with fresh mango in this popular Thai sweet.
It can be made with black or white glutinous rice.

INGREDIENTS

400ml coconut milk

½ cup chopped palm sugar

½ cup sugar

1 tsp salt, plus extra to serve

2 pandan leaves, tied in a knot

2 cups cooked glutinous rice (about
    400g) (page 100)

2 mangoes, peeled and sliced

2 tsp toasted black sesame seeds,
    to serve

Thick coconut sauce

200ml coconut milk

1 tbsp sugar

1 tsp cornflour, mixed with 1 tbsp cold
    water

METHOD

1 Mix the coconut milk, palm sugar, sugar, salt and
pandan leaves together in a medium saucepan and bring to
a simmer. Add the cooked glutinous rice, stir occasionally
for about 10 minutes until the rice is tender and the
consistency of loose porridge, then turn off the heat, cover
the pot and allow it to stand for 10 minutes.

2 For the coconut sauce, bring the coconut milk and sugar
to a simmer in a small saucepan, then stir in the cornflour
mixture. Remove from the heat and allow to cool and
thicken.

3 Serve the sticky rice topped with mango, scattered with
the sesame seeds, a little extra salt and the coconut sauce.

NOTES

For a crunchy texture, this sweet is traditionally scattered with mung bean
seeds, which are available from Asian grocers, but I find black sesame seeds
look and taste a bit nicer.

Palm sugar and ordinary white sugar are often used together in many
Southeast Asian desserts. The palm sugar provides a rich flavour but it is
not as sweet as white sugar.

This dish, together with some Chicken, Coconut and Galangal Soup (page
180), Thai Grilled Pork (page 201), Beef and Basil (page 82), Glutinous Rice
(page 100), and Pad Thai (page 45) would make a great Thai dinner party
for six to eight people.

SESAME BALLS

MAKES 10 BALLS PREPARATION TIME 25 MINS **COOKING TIME 15 MINS**

The name of this dish in Chinese actually means 'glutinous rice balls', but in my family we've always just called them sesame balls for obvious reasons. They look impressive and they're actually very simple to make.

INGREDIENTS

1 cup smooth Red Bean Paste (page 215)

2 cups glutinous rice flour

¼ cup sugar

¾ cup water

¼ cup sesame seeds

2 litres vegetable oil, for deep-frying

METHOD

1 Using wet hands, roll the red bean paste into smooth balls about 2cm in diameter and place on a tray.

2 Mix the glutinous rice flour, sugar and water into a smooth dough. Rest it, covered in plastic wrap, for 10 minutes, then pinch off large pieces of dough and flatten them into discs with your hands. Wrap the red bean paste balls with the dough and roll in the sesame seeds.

3 Heat the oil to 160°C and deep-fry the balls in batches for about 5 minutes each until golden and puffed to double their size. Serve immediately.

NOTES

You can use all kinds of fillings for these. A teaspoon of peanut butter is delicious, as is a piece of milk chocolate (or even a mixture of the two).

Use untoasted sesame seeds for coating the balls, as they will toast in the frying process.

Keep the dough thick as you wrap the balls of red bean paste. Although the balls will puff, there is no leavening agent like yeast or baking soda in it, so if the covering of dough is too thin it will lose its pleasant chewiness by crisping too much.

The glutinous rice flour contains no gluten so to be honest, I have no idea what resting the dough achieves. I just do it because that's what my grandma always said to do, and that's reason enough for me.

We might be at the end of this book but we're definitely not finished yet. Learning how to cook is a process that never really ends.

By now you should have discovered what excites you about Asian food - the kind of dishes you love, and the kind you want to learn more about.

Maybe you've found a taste for the flavours of northern Thailand, or perhaps the simplicity and clarity of Japanese cuisine has struck a chord. It might be that your family now loves what you can do with your wok.

More than anything, I hope that this book has made you want to explore Asian cuisines further and if you do, there's a lot of places you can go. Food can take you around the world, back in time, through a microscope, and even into the future - the best part is deciding where you want the adventure to take you.

Get in touch and let me know how you're going with it. There's lots more for us to learn together.

www.adamliaw.com
www.twitter.com/adamliaw
www.instagram.com/liawadam
www.facebook.com/AdamLiawFanPage

INDEX